CARRYING
the
MESSAGE

CARRYING
the
MESSAGE

MATTHEW SLATER

authorHOUSE®

AuthorHouse™
1663 Liberty Drive
Bloomington, IN 47403
www.authorhouse.com
Phone: 1-800-839-8640

First published by AuthorHouse   07/11/2011

ISBN: 978-1-4634-1863-2 (sc)
ISBN: 978-1-4634-1862-5 (dj)
ISBN: 978-1-4634-1864-9 (ebk)

Library of Congress Control Number: 2011910158

Printed in the United States of America

This book is dedicated to the still sick and suffering. I will always remember how painful it was for me. The best part is I will always remember how joyous it was to achieve sobriety. Stay strong and accept help when it is offered.

We all have the strength deep down inside to conquer this addiction, but we must work together.

Author's Note

I want to thank God for pulling me from the valley of the shadow of death. I would, most certainly, not be here if it weren't for His divine power. I must mention my family and friends who have stuck with me through my worst of times. I put many of you through a lot of heartache, and for that I am deeply sorry. What I will continue to do is go on Carrying the Message. I love you all.

Carrying The Message

1

February 8, 2008

Day One

I arrived at Phoenix Recovery Center at about 9:30 a.m. Paper work was filled out and family left. I then had to take a piss test and my luggage was searched for any unwanted items. A room was given to me with a roommate #10. Sat through several meetings throughout the day until 8:00 p.m. After every meeting, smoke 'em if you got 'em and different activities such as basketball, horseshoes, walking, throwing the football or reading/studying . . . yuk. Day by day schedule is very busy and will wear me out. You are also given chores and must sign-up for times you can make phone calls (only on Saturday for 10 minutes and family visits and friends on Sundays). There is also a laundry sign-up sheet for specific times. If you want your meals, you better eat or starve. There are always snacks available (cereal, apples, fruit, etc.) Spent most of Day 2 meeting every other addict and playing basketball.

Hello. My name is Matt and I am a recovering alcoholic. A heavy weight has been placed upon me to write this inspirational book.

I feel that this is part of God's plan for me. I have written this in an attempt to help others who may be suffering with the disease of addiction. As well, this book should be most helpful to those of you who know of someone that is, or has, suffered from alcohol or drug addiction. Briefly, I will be discussing how alcoholism has affected me on various levels of my life. Both physically and psychologically, alcoholism has taken its toll on my life, as well as those around me. For the protection of friends and family, I have opted to leave names out of this literature. Similarly, I have decided to leave many events out of this reading. This is primarily for my protection and others.

My childhood was a rather interesting time for me. I always had many friends, yet, I never really felt like I belonged. I knew that I was different from the others. I really cannot explain why I felt that way, except for the fact that I was extremely hyper and was always getting into trouble.

I grew up in Maryland not far from Annapolis in a strict Irish, Christian family. There is, though, a dash of German and a sprinkle of Polish in the lineage. Ah yes, the perfect ingredients for an alcoholic in the making. It has been an interesting ride with this kind of background!

My immediate family consists of an older brother and an older sister, along with my mother and father. My family comprises of hard working people, strong, yet fun loving. Dad was a head supervisor for a power plant in Baltimore. Mom worked in the school system. My brother was (is) in the Marine Corps (once a Marine, always a Marine) and my sister married young. I, however, was just a little hellion.

Although, having been brought up with fine morals, I would occasionally need to be reminded of these. Fondly, I remember this one particular event. My parents had caught me stealing from a local convenience store. The story began while I was venturing around the neighborhood. One day I met with a kid who was known, then, as being a troublemaker. We found this dusty, dirty path that led to a convenience store. Here, being eight years old, we were searching for trouble. My friend and I decided to walk into the shop and steal these baseball stickers. Now, back then, you would take these stickers and place them in an album. Seeing as baseball was my interest and true love at the time, it was only appropriate that I would steal these. All of the cool kids had these and I wanted to be the first to fill up my album. After our shoplifting duties were finished, we would hastily make our way back home. I was always careful to keep my bounty hidden because my parents were ever vigilant. Apparently, I was not sneaky enough. After some time, my folks began to realize that my sticker album was becoming full. They began asking each other how Matt was getting these stickers. They knew that I only received so much of an allowance. Well, my thieving days were coming to a direct halt. I was finally approached by my folks and I did not have an immediate explanation. They did manage to get a response from me the old school way. The old saying, "Spare the rod and spoil the child," was what they lived by. The way they wielded the "rod," could have shown the C.I.A. a trick or two about interrogation. Angrily, the very next day, my parents drove me back to the convenience store and made me apologize to the manager. This was so embarrassing, as it should have been, and I was banned from the store. Needless to say, this was a lesson learned and not forgotten.

My deviant behavior was now getting me into trouble in school. All through elementary and junior high, I was always starting a ruckus. I was suspended constantly for fighting, insubordination and just causing pure chaos. These behaviors, of course, were a huge concern of my parents. Because I was always causing a commotion in elementary school, my teachers would send me to the principal's office almost daily. Back then, teachers would issue "bubble sheets." Now, I believe they are commonly referred to as "referrals." Basically, it is paperwork stating that you are in big trouble. Along with the sheet, my parents would have to be contacted by phone every time. I cannot remember exactly how many "bubble sheets" one would have to receive in order to be suspended. Either way, I am quite sure that I far exceeded this amount regularly. If a day had gone by and I was not in the office, the principal, probably, assumed that I did not show up for school.

My folks could not figure out what to do. I am quite sure that I was putting a strain on their marriage. They tried punishment, medication and counseling, but nothing seemed to work.

One day they would introduce me to sports. Voila . . . the answer. What better way to vent all of this hyper energy? I played soccer very well; however, I quickly lost interest. After my first season, I decided to move on to baseball. Because of my incredibly high energy level, I tried bowling at the same time. I was developing into a well-rounded athlete.

Along with playing sports, I excelled in music. I learned to play the piano as well as the guitar. Eventually, the music scene faded away, but sports always remained with me.

Now, my first encounter with what soon became my newest hobby.

2

The first drink was on Christmas Eve when I was thirteen. There were family parties with my grandparents (who lived in Florida and would visit us at Christmas), close friends and other relatives. Being an Irish family, this was just normal behavior for me. While the adults were playing cards, socializing, drinking, laughing and just having a merry time, I was in the basement playing pool. Actually, I was developing into a pool shark at my young age. After shooting a game or two, one of the relatives entered the basement. Unknowingly, this was the time for me to be introduced to the start of my drinking career. He told me to have a beer, but drink it as fast as I could. So, being curious as to how it tasted, I obliged with zero resistance. I began to chug the beer until there was nothing left. I was handed yet another and I repeated this process once again. Carbonation and burps obviously followed. This, of course, was a foreign taste, but something magical happened. Suddenly, the strange taste didn't matter anymore.

It is hard to describe exactly what I felt but this feeling of numbness throughout my whole body began to take place, euphoria, if you will. This was it! I discovered my new love. In addition to having this new and exciting feeling, I was instructed to keep this event quiet. Do you honestly think that I would be able to conquer this task?

Shortly afterwards, as expected, I blew the secrecy as I tripped up the steps into the kitchen. With some of the family sitting in the kitchen and playing cards, why couldn't I have tripped down the steps? Looking like a deer caught in the head lights, I just felt my parents' eyes piercing through me. Quickly, I had to find an excuse. So with nothing intelligent to say, I simply said that I just tripped. Duh!!! My parents then asked, "So did you have enough to drink?" How was I supposed to respond to this question? Of course, I began to stammer over my response. For one, I was intoxicated and two, I was nervous. This of course was a double whammy for me. Surprisingly, enough, my folks just began to laugh and proceeded with their card game. Did I just escape punishment I asked myself? Were there no consequences for my actions?

Christmas passed and months followed but nothing much was said about the incident. Drinking was something that I would incorporate into my teenaged years. Playing pool, video games, sports and being rebellious were all added in with spirits of alcohol. I do not recall at that time ever really having a compulsion to drink . . . it was just fun. Hanging out with my friends, drinking and creating havoc just went hand and hand.

My days of boozing were quickly becoming a part of my juvenile existence. I did not realize, at this time, the magnitude of my irresponsible actions. Soon, this recklessness caught up to me this one particular day.

Suddenly, I am awakened to a loud and rather intense beeping noise. What is that? Where am I? Instinctively I throw my hands outward in a blind fury and began slapping in the direction of this obnoxious sound. I finally made contact with what I realized was my alarm clock. This was a head splitting melody. Lying in bed with my cotton mouthed, head pounding, friend of mine

(commonly referred to as a hangover), I began to wonder why my clock was ringing. With my head cloudy and still pulsating and everything still in a haze, I began to mentally retrace the steps from the night before.

Slowly, I remembered events from yesterday. I was in my room drinking Canadian whiskey from my stash and recalled hopping into my beat-up Volkswagen Rabbit and driving over to my cousin's house. About a half hour later, I arrived at his house and he hopped into my car. We proceeded to a liquor store that would always serve minors such as ourselves. This place was not exactly in the best of locations. We walked into the store and rounded up some malt liquor from the refrigerated section and then approached the counter. Without a second glance, the clerk decided to serve us. Victoriously, we proceeded to drive to a desolate spot underneath a bridge. After drinking and talking for a short time, the effects of the booze began thoroughly kicking in. We even helped someone jump start their car. After a couple of hours, drunk and behind the wheel, I proceeded to drive my cousin home.

I then began to remember navigating down the highway blasting my car stereo and feeling delightfully buzzed. Oh no!

Suddenly my thoughts came rushing in to my head like a dam that just burst. I had gotten arrested last night. I started to remember driving to my girlfriend's house. On the way, I was pulled over by the police. Just one more mile is all that I would have had to travel to reach my destination. I am now detained on the side of the road surrounded by police officers. Two officers then approached my vehicle and asked for my license and registration. I remember struggling to find my registration. One of the officers peered into my passenger's side and noticed that there were two full bottles of malt liquor on the floor. He then asked me, "What were you planning on doing with those?" Not thinking clearly, I told him that I was planning to drink them later. Yep, that did it! The next thing I know I am outside on the side of the road performing a field sobriety test. Naturally, I thought that I did well on the tests, even though, the officers had a different opinion. Then I was placed in handcuffs and transported to the police station with a blood alcohol content of 0.17, and way over the limit.

After a couple of hours of processing and frequent trips to the bathroom to relieve myself, the officers called my parents. I would have rather stayed in jail. Disappointed, my folks picked me up and took me back home. As of now, I do not have a license anymore because it was confiscated by the police. I began thinking to myself, "How can I get to college today, yet alone baseball practice?" "Will I have to drop out of college and quit the team?" "How will I pay for the court costs, fines and attorney fees?" "Did I call my girlfriend back last night?" "If I did call her, what did I say?"

What a way to wake up in the morning. Needless to say, that was definitely a huge wake-up.

With my folks disappointed in me, as they should be, I then had to make some huge lifestyle changes. I don't know if any of you have ever had the luxury of receiving a D.W.I. If so, then you can most certainly relate to how much of a headache they produce. For a teenager it was hell! I attempted to finish my first semester at the local community college. I was receiving car rides back and forth to class. This of course did not last long.

One day, while sitting in English class, I began feeling rather nauseous. Suddenly, I could not catch my breath and began to panic. My body started to become numb and my fingers started to shrivel up into a fist. My heart was pounding violently and I became very dizzy. Stumbling out of the class room and down the halls, I luckily found the nurses' station. The nurses sat me down and called the paramedics. Before I knew it, I was in the ambulance being transported to the hospital. Later, I found that I had suffered an anxiety attack. This was very terrifying.

I was eventually released from the hospital with a brown bag souvenir. The staff had instructed me on its proper usage. They told me that whenever I felt an attack coming, just breathe slowly into the bag. Surely this would work, considering my whole body will begin to spaz while trying to take slow breaths. I followed the doctor's orders and I eventually learned how to calm myself down.

Apart from the panic attack, I now had to drop out of college. My transportation back and forth to school was no longer available. What really bothered me the most was that I had to quit the baseball team, especially, since I was one of the starting pitchers. Well, the responsibility aspect was now beginning. Responsibility? What is that? I found out rather quickly, as I now prepared for my D.W.I. court appearance.

My life was now beginning to go through some drastic changes. I now had to get my first real job and figure out how I was going to get back and forth to work. Because of not having a license to drive, my social life suffered. I was pretty much on house arrest under my parents' watchful eyes. The only things for me to do at home were to play basketball, lift weights, and sit on the pier. This, for a teenager like me, was brutal. I should be out with my friends driving and going to places, right? This of course took a toll on my emotions, but I put myself in this predicament.

Eventually, my day in court had finally arrived. My parents and I showed up at the Juvenile Court in Annapolis along with my attorney. I, of course, pled guilty to my charge. The judge gave me probation before judgment. This means that if I were to have broken the law in any way within a year of this date, I would then be fully charged for this D.W.I. Just the same, I would have been charged for the most current offense as well. This was only a portion of my sentence. Because of the severity that goes with a D.W.I. charge, I now had to attend a drug and alcohol class. The judge also ordered me to visit the Shock Trauma Center in Baltimore City. Have any of you have ever seen the scared straight television program that was aired years ago? Scared straight was a show where a cast member would take troubled teens to a prison.

They would have the inmates scare the life out of them in an attempt to prevent them from future incarceration. Well, my visit to shock trauma was along the same lines. It was a rather gruesome experience, to say the least.

The nurses would walk a group of us around the critically injured people. Then the nurses began to explain to us what had happened to these people and why they were here. Anyway, I never thought that the sight of blood would faze me. I mean, I had seen plenty of horror and "slasher" movies before. I should be used to this. Right? I was very mistaken. It was the most terrifying, bloody, and disturbing scene that I had ever experienced in my short-lived lifetime.

I was intently staring at these victims with their blood dripping off the sides of their soon to be death beds. This was making me extremely nauseous. Puddles of blood were forming all over the floor as other nurses and doctors were running frantically to aid these victims. I do remember in particular a man lying down with a horde of bed sheets over top of his chest down to his torso. These sheets were soaked in blood. The staff had to swap out these sheets every five minutes only to keep replacing them. I was told the reason for this was because he had been shot 16 times. Apparently, this man was high on PCP and thought that it would be entertaining to grab his girlfriend by her legs and bash her skull on the side walk. This man bludgeoned her head one too many times and her brains gushed out all over the street. Two pedestrians had witnessed this atrocious scene and unloaded sixteen shots from their handguns into this man. We were then told, "When the PCP wears off, he will die."

As you can imagine, I was beginning to get sick and almost passed out. I left the hospital later that day and never wanted to see it again. I have decided to share this part of my story because it was a life changing scene.

Besides the classes and my horrific shock trauma experience, I also had to fight with the Maryland Motor Vehicles Administration. In an attempt to get my license back, I attended a hearing. Apparently, the arresting officer in my case was found negligent on a few different procedural policies. I should have been given a temporary license almost immediately after I had been arrested. After repeated phone calls to the police barracks, in an attempt to speak to my arresting officer, he never replied. Because of this event, I was left without a license for roughly seven and a half months. During the hearing with the M.V.A., they took this into consideration. Instead of receiving another seven months or so without a license, the M.V.A. only gave me another 27 days. This was great news because, in less than a month, I would be getting my license back. After receiving the license again, I re-entered the world of boozing. You think I would have learned my lesson by now? Well, I learned that I was not going to drink and drive anymore . . . at least, I thought.

A few weeks later, a buddy of mine decided to stop by my house with some malt liquor and cheap wine. Being as we were still teenagers, the cheaper the better. What did we care? We were hanging out in my room and decided that we were going to start drinking. Keep in mind that I had not had one drop of alcohol for those seven months due to frequent testing. I did not realize that my tolerance level had dropped. We proceeded to pound our drinks and, wow, I had gotten torn up. After a couple hours or so, my friend went home. I remember sitting down on my bed with my head just spinning. I figured that maybe I should just sleep it off. Lying down in bed, staring at the ceiling, my room took on a moving sensation like the swaying of a boat. I knew that I had to throw the anchor down. The anchor was my leg being planted on the floor in an attempt to stop this nauseating motion.

Anyhow, I woke up the next morning with an all too familiar feeling. I had plenty of hangovers before that day, and, yet I never seemed to enjoy them. Apparently, I had gotten sick overnight. I blacked out and didn't remember vomiting all over the side of the house. My father was outside mowing the lawn that next morning and noticed my funk. It was all over the siding of the house, outside of my window. After an hour or so of cleaning my funk, my parents were now fully aware of my trip back to trouble land.

Alcohol and I were now partners in crime. When I say crime, I mean this literally. Alcohol and younger people for the most part equals trouble. I am going to explain only a tiny portion of the chaos that I stirred up during my youthful drinking.

3

At this point in time, I was somewhere in my late teens. I wish that I could tell you exactly how old I was but these were very confusing times for me. I was an excellent baseball player who had major league scouts interested in me. I traveled to different states, playing ball and partied much more. Even though my passion was baseball, alcohol was my love.

My party life came, however, first on the priority list. Drinking was a way of loosening up and getting out of myself for a while. I was always very critical of me and constantly pursued perfection in everything (My parents were both perfectionists so I'm guessing that this rubbed off on me.). Despite my aforementioned D.W.I., it did not stop me from drinking and riding. My friends would pick me up whenever we were going out to get hammered. That was about 90% of the time. What really makes this disturbing is that my friends would drink and drive anyway. We were all just plain nuts and adding alcohol to the picture was just flat-out insane.

We would go to many parties during the weekend and a couple, occasionally, on the week days. Taking a trip to our infamous, underage serving liquor store was undoubtedly a weekly priority. Many times, my friends and I would travel there in packs.

It was usually four of us to a car. After we would purchase the booze, we would stuff the cases of beer in the trunk. We did make sure that we had something to drink inside of the car as well. This would now begin the inevitable chaos.

I do remember a party in particular that my friends and I decided to crash. I was riding shotgun in one of my friend's car. As we were driving through this neighborhood in search of the party, we heard this loud bang. Apparently, this guy that I used to know from high school decided to kick my buddy's car as we were driving. I had always disliked this person because of disagreements in the past. What a bad time it was for this guy to initiate trouble because at this point I had already been boozing and was feeling crazy. Suddenly, my buddy proceeded to slam on his brakes and I hopped out of the passenger seat with a "ready to use" baseball bat. Keep in mind; I was one of the best hitters in the state.

Therefore, I decided to give chase after this guy. While running, I had taken a walloping swing at him. Being a soccer player and faster, he ran out of my reach. I disliked this guy so much from school that I really wanted a piece of him. Looking back, if I had struck him, he could have been killed or seriously injured. At that point in time, though, it would have been perfectly fine with me. My friends started to yell for me from the car to get back in. So, I hopped into the passenger's side. Influenced by alcohol, we gave chase with my buddy's car knowing that he was retreating to a nearby party.

When all five of us pulled up to the party, sure enough, we noticed him scampering into the house. We decided to get out of the car, leaving the bat behind. As we entered the party, almost instantly, it became apparent that we were not welcome. The guy that I was chasing had stormed out the back door of the house. At this time, I had no clue that he left. We were determined not to leave until we found this guy. People at the party were not agreeing with our decision and started to become hostile toward us. I proceeded to push and shove my way through the mob when this other guy confronted me. He decided that he was going to play the hero and put himself face to face with me. Having been an athlete in tip top shape, I gave our hero one warning to get out of my face, but he did not oblige. With my adrenaline pumping, I proceeded to pick this punk up off his feet and throw him backwards. He hit the ground and did a couple head-to-toe flips. To me, it was rather humorous to watch him flip over like a gymnast doing somersaults. I am guessing that he didn't see the humor in this. Shortly afterwards, he stood up and began to make his way out of the party. Surprisingly enough, the crowd then decided to let me through with no resistance at all. Since I could not find the person who kicked the car, we abandoned our search and left to cause trouble elsewhere.

Later the next day, I started asking myself questions. What was I thinking? What if I actually did find this guy? What would I have done to him in that current state of mind? I was always quick to shrug off these questions. The truth is as long as they kept making alcohol, I just didn't care.

On another evening, three of us were drinking and driving downtown and decided to take a walk around in hopes of finding some girls. I am feeling really tight at this point from drinking. That crazy feeling inside of me began again. This would frequently happen when becoming inebriated. Being pumped up and ready to fight, I began "gabbing off" to my friends about a subject of mild importance. While drunk and not really caring about my use of profanity, a crowd nearby overheard my cursing. This guy approached me and assumed that I was directing my foul language at him. He was all dressed up, looking like a "want to be" thug (I am sure that most of us have had the luxury of meeting these people at some point). He was wearing a gold chain around his neck that looked like it came from the Mr. T starter set. His hat was on sideways and he spoke with that annoying, fake accent. This guy was one of those punks that I just despised. At any rate, he decided to approach me. In a smug manner he then asked if I was talking to him. Even though I wasn't, I wanted to rumble. I then replied, "Yes, I was. What are you going to do about it?" Immediately, this crowd of seven began running at us. My first reaction was to take Mr. T out, who was still in front of me. I remember rocking back while clenching my right fist. I then threw a punch so swiftly that it must have looked like my fist was being launched from a sling shot. I definitely hit my target with precise accuracy. I popped this guy square in the nose and watched him drop to the ground in a hurry. At that time I realized that I split his nose rather violently. Can you visualize a sprinkler spitting blood across your lawn as opposed to water? This is pretty much what this guy looked like. With this guy down for the count, two others came running at me. I figured that I may as well go down swinging. After some punches being exchanged from both sides, I decided to hit the ground. I began to cover my head while these guys started kicking me in the ribs. Surprisingly enough, I do not remember feeling any of it. Alcohol seemed to have taken care of that problem. I glanced over to my left and my one buddy was lying on the ground grimacing in pain. My other friend was sitting down and didn't lend a hand. Needless to say, my other friend and I didn't talk much after this incident.

I heard sirens and the police were racing to get here. The guys who were kicking me halted and then took off running. After some effort, I pulled myself up and managed to get my buddy off of the ground. Then, we started to sprint as fast as we possibly could. As we were running from the police, a couple girls decided to join the chase. All three of us, including these girls, managed to sneak in between buildings and houses eluding the police.

Apparently, these girls were dating the guys to whom we were fighting. They informed us that these guys were in a dangerous gang that had been causing mayhem in the area for a while now. This did not stop us that night from carrying on with the drinking though. When I woke up the next morning, I had almost forgotten about the fight completely. The next day, my friend who had gotten the worse of the fight, called me. After I drove over to his house and saw his horrid looking face, we began plotting revenge. Still upset about what had happened the previous evening, I began to rally the troops.

Ten of us decided to head downtown the next night and settle this once and for all. To our dismay, they never showed up.

I read in the newspaper, not long after this event, these guys had been arrested and sent to jail for their prior crimes. Looking back now, I have asked myself what would have happened if they had possessed guns or knives? What if the police caught us? Booze, once again, played a detrimental factor in my decision making. Still I just didn't see it. I had most definitely become a problem drinker.

On occasion I would reflect upon my prior actions. I would ask myself, "Who am I?" I am not the same person that my folks had raised. I had no respect for authoritative figures in any way, shape or form. I was always engaging in fights because I somehow enjoyed them.

At one point, I even went after an off duty police officer. The officer was drunk and had started a fight with me by pelting my car with a tennis ball. He said that I was driving too fast down the street. Afterward, I drove up the street and grabbed my friends that were at a local party. We came back and chased the officer back into his house. Eventually, the on-duty police arrived and apologized for his actions. But, we just didn't care.

Family and friends would often say to me, "Hey, man, you should slow down your drinking." Because I was, of course, in denial thinking that alcohol had anything to do with my actions, I would just blow them off and move on.

As time went on and months passed, I was still up to my old antics. Drink after drink, fight after fight, girl after girl. I had grown increasingly worse. Around this time, I been shot at and then decided that it would be a good idea to purchase a gun.

Hence, I bought myself a brand new 20 gauge, single shot, shotgun. It was the easiest thing in the world to buy. I had to be 18 years of age with a clean criminal record. Surprisingly, through all of this, I was able to keep my background spotless. My D.W.I. was the only red flag. I did not realize how insane I was at that time.

The shotgun remained in my car at all times. Along with the gun, I, subsequently, purchased a machete and kept it underneath my passenger's seat. Here I am walking the streets, not mentally stable, armed with life taking weapons, what in the world was I thinking? Actually I wasn't thinking. My judgment was so impaired by my addiction that I couldn't make sense of anything. Thankfully my shotgun was confiscated by the police before I was at my worst.

Next, I began hanging with people just as crazy, if not worse. Some of these people were doing cocaine, heroin, drinking and smoking weed. I really did not give much thought to my future. I always knew that I was very talented in baseball and would one day play in the minors, at least. Because of the major league scouts and publicity that I was receiving, my ego was getting higher. I didn't pay much attention to the scouts when they suggested to me that I should go to a college of their choosing. I will make it to the majors regardless of college. Thus, with that in mind, I proceeded to carry on with my reckless ways.

With every drink, my hopes and dreams of becoming a professional baseball player were fading away.

My lifestyle was catching up to me in a hurry. Some of the people that I was associating with were getting arrested for theft, fighting with cops, drinking and driving, and drugs. Others that I knew died. After time, I began to realize that I needed to make some changes in my life. I then decided to move on. Even though, I left everyone from that life style, alcohol was still the friend of mine that I took with me.

4.

My new change in attitude and lifestyle was certainly an improvement. Nevertheless, I still continued to hurt others throughout this process. When I was younger, I hardly ever took the time to evaluate my life and where it was heading. Becoming so self-centered and manipulative, I never gave much thought as to who I was hurting or affecting with my actions. All that I seemed to care about was me. I would lie to your face if I knew that it would benefit me.

Since I had become so accustomed to the partying lifestyle, I would often stay out all night. This took a heavy toll on my family. I would normally crash on the couch at a buddy's house or stay at a girlfriend's house. I was hardly ever able to drive home, considering that I was constantly tanked. On many occasions, I would stay out several nights at a time and would not call home.

Whenever I needed money or I was in a tight spot, my folks were always there for me. They always prevailed. Likewise, they were always concerned for my well-being. Yet, I couldn't see it. I would argue with them constantly over my questionable decisions. All of this arguing made me want to drink even more. I became rebellious, gave up on my baseball career, and armed myself with a horde of excuses as to why. The fact is that drinking was now more important to me than ever.

I began drinking over everything. I would drink on days that ended with "y." It didn't matter if it was sunny, rainy or snowy. There was always an excuse to drink. If I was happy and excited or down and depressed, you could find me with a bottle in my hand. I had incorporated alcohol into almost every activity. I loved the way it made me feel, numbing my nerves, especially, if I were worried or stressed over something.

Even so, my folks still let me stay at their house. I had become very dependent upon them because I could not afford my own place (Imagine that!). I was working at a dead end pizza shop and scrapping to make my car payments. In actuality, I was spending at least half of my earnings on booze. When my shifts were over, I would venture out to parties and college campuses. From there, I would just get annihilated. Now keep in mind that I am still in my late teens.

Further arguing would ensue between my parents and me. Questions would continuously rise to the surface. What are you going to do with your life? Where is all your money going? Why didn't you call to let us know that you are still alive?

These arguments made my blood boil. I did not want to hear any of this stuff, especially, when my head was throbbing from the night before. I would think to myself: Why do they care where my money is going? I am now an adult so why should I have to call them? Why are they treating me like a child?

Well, I did some soul searching and came up with answers to these questions. When I actually slowed myself down enough to think logically, it had become quite obvious. I still live under their roof. Maybe, just maybe, they really do care about my well—being. Now the question I began to ask myself was: "How can I now keep living this lifestyle and keep my parents happy at the same time?"

This was going to have to be performed delicately. Since I was younger, I had mastered the art of manipulation. Having been a very persuasive person, I was very good at convincing people to do just about anything for me. Probably, I could have talked someone out of their shoes. I hated having to do this, particularly, to those I loved. But in order for alcohol and I to continue our relationship, manipulation was the way to go.

I would often lie and convince my folks to lend me some money. Often I would come up with a most elaborate story in hopes that they would sympathize with me. By doing this, I would benefit financially or for other reasons. Often times I would lie about where my money was going. I really did cause my family a lot of grief. Apparently, I had chosen a path of destruction all due to the blinding effects of alcohol.

As time went on, I continued to cause financial anguish for my parents. I was still borrowing money and feeding them lame excuses. My car would eventually break down and, of course, I did not have the money to fix it. My parents recognized that if I did not have an operational vehicle then I could not make it to work.

So, in turn they would lend me enough money for repairs. I would pay my folks back on occasion.

As you may have guessed, I was in denial over my drinking. I never stopped running long enough to see that my life was in chaos. Even if I did stop, I would have had to get honest and examine my life and problems. But, there was no way I would have wanted to do that. I was beginning to despise myself because of who I was becoming. I would see so many people maintain a lifestyle similar to mine, but could drink every day and still keep healthy relationships. How did they do that? Deep down inside I wanted that for myself. Through repeated attempts, this feat could not be accomplished. Consequently, I continued to strain my relationships with my parents and other family members.

My parents knew that I was definitely not an angel. What often worried them were the people that I chose to hang out with. Some of the girls that I would associate with became a problem in the household. I remember one girl in particular that my mother just could not tolerate. Now, mothers are usually selective over who is going to date their children anyway. For some reason this girl had really gotten beneath my mother's skin. Naturally, my mother and I began to butt heads over my choice. She would plead and plead for me not to date this girl. Of course, I insisted that she just needed to respect my judgment. After a good twenty minutes or so of arguing back and forth, I was becoming extremely angry. I was then given an ultimatum from my mother. She said that either I stop dating this girl or I could find another place to live. Both of us were in the basement of the house at this time. I was standing next to our fireplace. As I began to feel my temper rising and my blood boiling, I proceeded to do something stupid. Grabbing the glass door, that was attached to the brick in the fireplace, I, in a fit of rage, ripped the door from the bricks. Pieces of brick had started tumbling from the fireplace. My mother's eyes lit up in fear. Mom proceeded to run up the stairs from the basement and looked for my father. As I was standing there, I had not remembered, ever being that angry. Needless to say, a couple minutes later my folks instructed me to pack my bags and get out.

This ritual of packing my bags and getting out became a reoccurring situation with my folks. Having to live place to place, I just couldn't seem to make it on my own. All the while, I kept drinking and living a most unhealthy lifestyle. Why couldn't I understand why I was not able to make ends meet?

Many of my relationships had faltered due to my abuse of alcohol. Some alcoholics or problem drinkers tend to be physically abusive towards their loved ones. On the other hand, I was just the opposite. I was a very mentally abusive drunk. At a young age, I was taught to never put my hands on a female. Guess that I was absent for the mentally abusive lecture, though.

Before I had become a problem drinker, I was mostly polite and genuine, very well mannered, organized and full of self-assurance. I was the kind of person that people wanted to be around. Even though, having felt different from others, I still enjoyed their company.

Mothers on occasion would ask me if I would be interested in dating their daughters. Wow, if I only had that suggestion now.

Being an active alcoholic in any relationship, is not healthy for either person. I had destroyed much companionship. Not only did I lose trust in my friends, family, and co-workers, but my girlfriends, as well.

In high school, I had a girlfriend with whom I had shared many experiences. We had dedicated much time to each other and had a lot in common. She was just a fantastic person. Not having been in a serious relationship before, we were both young and naive. People would have called it puppy love. After some time together, I figured that things were going well between us. But, she began acting strangely causing me to suspect that she was cheating. Knowing that she was not going to tell me directly that she was cheating, I decided to play a mind game with her. Eventually, I was able to trick her into confessing that my suspicions were confirmed. Never the less, I was crushed. Not only was my girlfriend cheating, but with one of my best friends. Ever since that day, relationship to relationship, I harbored anger and insecurity.

I began having commitment problems. With some girls, I truly did want to make things work out between us, but instead I would just run from commitment and straight to the bottle.

Eventually, I met this girl that just knocked me off of my feet. She was beautiful in every sense of the word. Our personalities meshed extremely well together. We would often have conversations on the phone for hours. Usually, I could not tolerate a conversation with some girls for more than five minutes. As time went on, we started to date and many great things between us began to escalate. I had taken her to meet my family and they adored her. Similarly, she introduced me to her family and they loved me as well. I began thinking, "Could this be the one?" Everything was just coming together so easily. Needless to say, we fell in love. I was holding down a great job at the time, as was she. I had to be extra careful this time because things were looking rather promising. I had slowed my drinking down for a while.

After dating for quite some time and things between us just kept getting better, I was able to limit my drinking times to weekends. I just could not picture myself with anyone else. At this point in time, I finally knew what I wanted. I wanted to ask for her hand in marriage. I couldn't believe that marriage was on my mind, yet alone I trusted her. With my background of insecurity in relationships, one would think that this was an impossible feat. Well, the proposal day was fast approaching. I had planned everything out on how I was going to propose. Somehow, I managed to organize this event perfectly. Finally, the day had arrived.

I had decided that I was going to ask her father for his daughter's hand in marriage. As I had hoped, her father eagerly accepted and was most supportive. I had contacted a limousine company and made arrangements for this special night. Likewise, I had made reservations for a rather exquisite restaurant.

After work that day, I had hurried over to her parents' house to await her arrival. When she had gotten home, I asked her to get dressed up. When she had asked why, I explained that we were going out to dinner. I think that she knew something was happening, but she played along. As she was sprucing up, the limo arrived. I can still remember the excitement in her facial expression. She then of course begged me to tell her where we were going. I just explained to her that it was a surprise. So, off in the limo we went.

After a short drive, she soon realized that we had arrived at the very same place where we had our first date at a beach, not far from where I grew up. After stepping out of the limo and taking a brief walk, I was very nervous. But, I think that I kept my composure. I knew that there was no better time than now to get down on my knee and propose to her. She began to cry tears of happiness as she answered yes. I, of course, was the happiest man alive. This was a day that I will never forget.

We then proceeded to the restaurant and had a lovely dinner. The rest of the night, I told her, was all hers. We had the limo driver take us to her parents' house, pick them up, and all of us rode around and celebrated the rest of the night. This night was very special and most memorable.

Shortly, thereafter, we had decided to get an apartment together. We had an agreement that she would stay some nights and the other nights with her parents. I was staying at the apartment full time, though. The waters, so to speak, were being tested to make sure that we were to be functional under the same roof.

Being engaged was quite an experience for me. Half of the time I was staying at my apartment by myself. But, I was beginning to grow agitated the closer we got to the wedding date. I began drinking heavily once more. After a brief amount of time, my drinking was becoming very noticeable. I started to drink more heavily and more frequently than I had in previous years. I had everything going my way and couldn't understand why I had chosen to do this. I had a beautiful fiancé, great job, and my own apartment. Still, I could not fight off the compulsion to drink.

She had begun to get worried, as well as our families. I started to doubt the marriage and myself. Mentally, I was losing it. I began to drink more and more in an attempt to mask my feelings. The wedding was almost completely paid for at this point. It was about a month away when I felt the pressure hit me like a speeding freight train. My drinking was beginning to rear its ugly head once more. Then, finally, out of the blue one day, I decided to make a shocking decision. I called off the wedding. Obviously, this did not go over well with her and her family. As you can imagine, when I broke the news to my fiancé, she was quite upset. She slammed her engagement ring on the counter, slammed the door, and walked out of my life. But, this was what I wanted. Right?

Deep down inside of me my answer was no. I still loved her, but my love for alcohol was much deeper.

As time went on, I continued down my reckless path. I had got involved in other relationships. Those, of course, ended badly, as well. I would get drunk despite the endless pleas from my girlfriends. For this reason, I just could not function in a relationship. I was verbally abusive to many because I was drunk all of the time.

This was not me. When drinking I would turn into a monster. Can you picture a person living in the same house as you with issues of fear, anger, denial, self-pity, and amplify that by three? Unfortunately, many people have lived with an untreated alcoholic and some still are. I can only imagine the hell that I put my friends, family, and co-workers through. I was becoming Dr. Jekyll and Mr. Hyde. Without the alcohol, I was a great guy. With the alcohol consumed, I was a monster.

In conclusion, alcohol ruined the majority of my relationships. Not just with girlfriends, but with everyone around me. I was a walking nightmare for many years. Looking back, now, I realize how tough it must have been for everyone. And for this I am truly sorry. Alcoholism took almost everything from me. This is a most deadly disease.

5

I want to discuss in this chapter just how devastating alcoholism can be while trying to maintain employment. I have had many jobs in the past. Some of these jobs were from when I was younger and simply just did not like them. Yet, many of my jobs I lost because of my struggle with alcoholism.

Over the years I had excelled in the field of Security/Law enforcement becoming a bounty hunter, as well as, a government contracted Security officer. Most of my experience, however, came from being a Loss Prevention detective or agent. As a loss prevention detective, my primary responsibility was to reduce theft. I worked in various retail chains protecting company assets.

We would all dress in ordinary clothing looking like a normal everyday shopper. The reason being was to disguise ourselves from thieves. We were tasked with many responsibilities, but most importantly, was the arresting of dishonest employees, as well as, shoplifters. The overall safety of shoppers and staff was also in our job description.

We had many ways of catching thieves. Having a sophisticated state of the art camera system always helped. We were able to record just about anything in the store digitally, 24 hours a day. Our cameras were so precise that I could zoom in on a shopper from one department to another and read the time on their watches. Because of this technology, as you could imagine, I had become accustomed to dealing with the public day to day.

Dealing with the public professionally, on a daily basis, was a necessary aspect of my job. So with that in mind, showing up to work with the stench of alcohol permeating through my pores was not very professional. Sure, a lot of people would go out and tag one on every now and then. But I was tagging it on at least five times a week. I would often attempt to disguise my breath with gum or mints. Looking like I just got stepped on was a bit harder to conceal.

For years I would roll into work almost always with a hangover of some sort. I could make it through the day without a problem. And, then after work, I would drink again. The cycle would then continue. I was always excellent at what I did on the job. I would win awards for catching the most shoplifters and dishonest employees in a month's time. I also won awards for overall improvement and employee of the month. In some way, I was still able to function well, at least for now.

For me catching a thief was a very easy task. Even to this day I can spot a thief from a mile away. However, this skill was not obtained overnight. The job definitely had an element of danger along with stress. Some people have what it takes and many do not. My job was mostly all about reading peoples' body language. While I was busy reading other peoples body language, my co-workers were reading mine.

Everyone that I worked with could tell that I was a heavy drinker. I lost a lot of respect from them because of this. I was quick to make risky decisions at work, putting my staff on edge. Although my choices were a bit chancy, they always worked out in the end. All the same, it made most of my co-workers not want to work with me. You would think that I would have gotten a clue when all of them wanted to rearrange their schedules so they could work with someone else. The funny thing about this situation is that my bosses knew I was a liability. Since I performed at a very high level, they would tend to overlook my problem. This of course would frustrate my co-workers but what could you do?

Later, my drinking had finally started to catch up with me. Being frequently late for work had now become a huge obstacle. I was now drinking so much from the night before that I couldn't seem to get up in the morning. Even when I did somehow get up, I could not function. I would feed myself all kinds of excuses. I would convince myself that it was because I was just getting older. I knew that something had to be done. I made a decision to try and control my drinking. I, now, will only drink on the nights that I do not have to work the next day. Needless to say, I tried, but to no avail. It did not workout according to plan.

I would continue to stumble into work with blood shot eyes, wrinkled clothing, and my breath smelling like a brewery. I was disheveled at times. I would look like someone ran me over with a truck and then duct taped my eye lids to my cheeks. I probably looked like someone who had just been through a C.I.A. interrogation. Working the camera systems at work just made me even more nauseous. Spinning the cameras around on the screens was a rather undesirable responsibility while experiencing a hangover.

After a few hours of work and some greasy food, I would normally begin to feel somewhat better. At times, my hangovers would last my whole shift. With all of my lateness's and occasional call outs from work, I was still determined to drink afterwards.

On and on this insane cycle would continue. My job performances began taking nose dives for the worse. Occasionally, I would fall asleep in the camera rooms. I was no longer the top dog at any of my jobs. I was now being written up for continuous lateness's and call outs. Losing job after job because of this vicious cycle, I became very unreliable and was now working just to feed my habit.

Because I kept losing jobs, I made excuses to my family by telling them that my position at work was cut or everyone on the staff had been fired because of an incident. My life was now full of stress. All along I was just in denial about my drinking. Alcoholism is a very mysterious disease when it has its grips on you.

I became much like a tornado destroying everything and everyone in my path by spinning and causing more damage and grief to those around me. Being clever, so I thought, I decided that I would work two jobs. By doing this, my drinking will slow down for sure. Well I went out and landed a part time job slinging pizzas. My two job theory began to work for a little while. Maybe this was it? I'm guessing that I must have had too much time on my hands before. I always remembered that saying: "An idle mind is the devils playground." I got it now. I will just keep my mind busy.

Shortly thereafter, I had moved drinking back into my busy schedule. I started to call out of my part time job because it was cutting into my drinking time. That's not fun! Eventually, I decided to quit that job because drinking was now a higher priority.

My family's disappointment in me grew stronger. They would often make suggestions to me like: "Why don't you join the military? Since you lack discipline they will teach it to you." "Maybe you just need a foot up your butt." "Maybe you should go back to school?" "If you do go back, you're paying for it though." "You can't seem to finish anything." "You work at dead end jobs and you're going nowhere." "You need a real job." "What happens if you get sick? You do not have medical insurance." "What do you want to do with your life?" Instead of me taking these questions and remarks as constructive criticism, I took immediate offense. I would ensue drinking more and more. I began to feel like a loser and would become depressed and often think that I will never be anything. I can't even hold a job.

My organizational skills were deeply troubled. I had a hard enough time deciding what I was going to drink that day, yet alone what I was going to wear.

My hangovers now had become increasingly worse. I began drinking heavier than normal. In a day, I could consume a case of beer. Other days I could drink two fifths of whiskey, an amount that could potentially kill the average drinker. I now realized that I had a problem with drinking, but I was not an alcoholic. Yes. I was in total denial.

Since my hangovers were almost completely intolerable, I had to do something. I decided one day that I would try to drink them away. To my surprise this worked. The "hair of the dog" is what many like to call this. In the mornings before work, I would often chug three or four beers. I would then hop in the shower feeling like a million bucks. Because of the depletion of alcohol in my body overnight, I would wake up in the morning with the "Shakes." My body was craving alcohol and was beginning to detoxify. So, I would simply just add more alcohol to my body to balance out these shakes. This certainly helped me to get to work on time. Questions would be asked to why I smelled like booze. I would often tell my co-workers that I just had a rough night. This excuse became acceptable most of the time. This style of drinking I liked to call "Maintenance Drinking."

Eventually, this caught up with me. I found that a couple of beers before work only made me crave more throughout the day. I began feeling sick in the middle of my work day. A couple of drinks on the job would be sufficient enough to patch me over. This for me at the time was a living hell. I had this whole other lifestyle that I kept hidden. On my lunch breaks I would sometimes drive to the liquor store and purchase a couple of miniatures of vodka. I would occasionally go to a nearby restaurant and have a Jack in Coke.

Now, I was drinking on the job but not every day. I was hiding from my feelings of self-pity and depression. I felt worthless and did not seem to care much about anything or anyone. I was so upset because I couldn't achieve anything positive in my life. How could I have stooped this low?

In the end, I eventually became unemployable. All of my bridges I had burned completely to ashes. My friends, family, and employers did not trust me anymore. Employers who were interested in me began to wonder why I only stayed with a company for three months or less. I had finally drunk myself into a corner.

I always knew in the back of my mind that I would eventually have to call out of work. My drinking habits would almost certainly force me to. Some alcoholics can function day to day making it to work. I was not a functional alcoholic.

I had an uncle who was a fully functional alcoholic. He retired from his job and was known for years as an excellent employee. Some alcoholics have this ability. Eventually, his drinking had caught up with him and he passed away at a reasonably young age.

After I had lost job after job and was scrapping for enough change to pay my bills, reality would occasionally set in. I do not have a job so I can't pay my bills. I could afford my alcohol though. Bill collectors began calling me non-stop and threatening me. My heart would race if they called me. All that I had to do was drink and they would go away. I would put my cell phone on silent and then drink myself into a stupor. My credit was perfect for years and I would always pay off my debts without a problem. My drinking took me for broke however. My drinking had put me into so much financial fear that it was almost unbearable. I had lost many things along the way. I had lost two apartments, jobs, girlfriends, credit, faith and trust of both family and friends. Eventually, I lost my mind.

Becoming sick or seriously injured was something that I would worry about all of the time. I did not have medical benefits for most of my alcoholic career. I could not hold a job long enough to receive benefits. If I were to have gotten sick or hurt, where would I have gotten the cash? I could have tried my folks but they were all used up with me at this point.

6

The most dangerous aspect of drinking for me was isolation. Isolation for me developed into an almost obsessive habit. The heaviest drinking that I had ever done was when I was alone. I had become comfortable not being around other people. With my emotions spinning around like a carousel, being alone seemed to favor me the most. Granted I could have spent hours at the local watering hole but it was far cheaper to drink at home. By doing this, I could also avoid many social encounters. It is strange looking back at these times because growing up I was never anti-social. I had slowly become reclusive.

Isolation was the last phase of my drinking. Being isolated can be the most deadly phase for an alcoholic. I would hide out in my room mostly during my darkest and final days of drinking. Hours upon hours it was just consuming the life out of me. All that I had for entertainment was a television and computer. This had become my command central of all social activity. I was becoming extremely depressed. My friend's whisky and beer helped to assist my depression. Don't get me wrong I did enjoy the company of wine, vodka, and rum. Now, I did make it out almost every day. Usually this effort involved driving to the liquor store or a relative's house. My trips to my relatives' houses were normally to raid their liquor cabinet. I would, frequently, make it to work only if it did not interfere with my three or four a day benders.

Nevertheless, I was beginning to hate my life. I was just becoming emotionally numb. Nothing really excited me anymore. I had reached the lowest of my lows. I didn't care about anyone or anything. No one knew just how far I had delved into my saddened state of mind. My attitude towards people was ice cold and bitter. It was however a frightening feeling when I became numb to almost everything. My mind was full of hate, anger, sadness, self pity, and fear. Lets just say that if I were someone else than I would have been scared of me. In retrospect, I really was someone else, not the carefree, fun, polite, courteous, and trustworthy person that I used to be. I had now become a walking nightmare. My life had become one as well, and yet I could not drink it away.

While I was in this sickened condition, I was drinking so much that I would hardly eat at all. Everything I ate my body would have a hard time digesting. Besides if I did eat too much then it would take away the effect that I was longing for. It was that feeling of euphoria that would take me away from reality.

My sister's house had a pier. There is just something magical about the water. I guess, while sitting there, I could find enough peace and tranquility to get away from me for a moment. During which time, crying was a frequent activity. My life had gradually taken a complete 180°. So much of my time was spent just pondering over my life and choices made. I would harshly criticize myself over decisions that could have been better.

Having been depressed so much, I didn't want to go on anymore. These emotional issues, for way too long, made me want to end my life, as I reflected upon all the people that I had hurt along the way. Remaining vividly in my mind were all of the relationships that had faltered along the way, as well as jobs. My financial situation was now looking grave. I had lost trust in my friends and family. The future was looking very dim and unpromising. I was very close to rock bottom.

I would often fall asleep at night in hopes that I would not wake up. I was drinking so much now at that the alcohol would permeate through my pores while I was sleeping. I would fear waking up in the middle of the night with the shakes. Sometimes, there were horrible anxiety attacks from drinking too much. After being weak from heavy drinking, the anxiety would hit me full force. Trying to calm your breathing down while you are shaking is no easy task. This living hell existed of hours of continual shaking, unending stress and nights of sleeplessness. There were many nights of dizzy spells, exhausting a dreary me to sleep. Spells would happen so quickly that I would almost jump out of bed.

Existing had become pure torture. Never in my life had I endured so much pain both physically and emotionally. I would pray to God at night while lying in bed and would often ask Him to just take me home. My body was spent and my tank was empty and I wanted out of this life. Suicide was not an option. I was now stuck because I couldn't kill myself and I wouldn't die. Looking back, I am grateful that I was raised in a Christian household. If not so, I probably would have gone right down to the local gun shop . . . shotgun would have done the trick. The really disturbing thing is that I had actually planned how I was going to take my life. How selfish would that have been? All the same I didn't care about me or anyone at that point. By knowing the Lord, personally, made me realize that there was no alternative, but to trust and continue living.

The Lord did not answer my prayers those nights, deciding to keep me alive. Apparently, part of His plan was to bring me back to sobriety. I am now very grateful that I am here and was given another chance at life and will keep carrying the message so that others who need help can hear this.

As a whole, looking back at my most unhealthy lifestyle, there was the most important spiritual factor lacking. I had forgotten about God, or rather at times pushed Him out of my life or avoided Him purposely. I was almost completely spiritually and emotionally bankrupt. Being in this state of mind is how so many alcoholics never see the happiness and joy of recovery.

I want to discuss what little faith I had left that saved me from certain death. It was late January leading into February. They were the most unforgettable final four days of my last bender. I had been low on hope, spirituality, and any ounce of sanity. Fear, anger, loneliness, and depression took over my life. My rock bottom had arrived. Binge drinking was my forte. And this morning, in particular, I remember because it was the most painful, physically and emotionally.

Staggering out of bed that morning and shaking violently, I thought that I would just keep drinking. Assuredly, I will begin to feel better. This trick usually worked plenty of times in the past but not so much this day. I began drinking the beer that I had stashed for occasions like this one. Having drunk three or four in succession, I figured that my shakes would go away and I would be ready to go once more. I then decided to hop in the shower because hot water would always relax me and sometimes help clear my head a bit. Unfortunately, the shower and the booze just did not seem to work. Still shaky and now feeling even more nauseous and dizzy, I felt like someone was flushing my head down the toilet. I remember asking myself, "Will these shakes go away soon or is something else wrong with me?" Panic took over and I proceeded to raid the liquor cabinet. There were so many different choices of hard liquor to choose from. I had opted to try them all. Eventually, my shakes would go away right? In this case they just would not banish.

I had now consumed so much alcohol that, to this day, I could not tell you exactly how much. It was an abnormally high amount. Depression grew stronger. A little voice in my head was telling me to end my life. Instinctively, I knew that I was now in serious turmoil. The chain of events that happened next I can only say was an act of God.

Being alone, depressed, and scared, I decided to call my sister on her cell phone. Usually, my sister would never answer her cell phone, especially if I was calling her. She was the kind of person who would check the number first and then call back. Nevertheless, I had to make the attempt. To my surprise she answered her phone. I hastily asked her to come pick me up because I was about to drink myself to death. I just could not stop drinking everything in the house. I truly believed that I had gone mad. In a panic mode, she told me that she would be right over. That alone was a miracle all in itself.

Not long after we ended our phone conversation she had arrived. She picked me up and was going to take me back to her house to get sober, but needed to stop by the gas station first. At this point, the only thing I cared about was having another drink. Shortly after we arrived at the gas station, I knew that this place sold alcohol. Secretly, I proceeded into the shop and purchased a pint of vodka. I was quick to conceal it in my jacket pocket. I then ventured back to the car and sat back down. My sister did not even realize that I had gone into the shop.

After fueling her car, we started down the road. Through discussion she had begun telling me about her concerns for me. I of course told her about how much I hated my life and that I didn't want to go on. This worried her. While we were still talking, I pulled the pint from my pocket and began to slam it as quickly as possible. I almost consumed the whole bottle. My sister, naturally, began to freak out. Not long afterwards, I was beginning to become very hostile. In a panic, my sister called a good friend that was a paramedic and explained the situation to him. He informed her that I needed to get to a hospital immediately. Because of my insane behavior, at this point, he had arranged for younger and stronger paramedics to come to my aid. The rendezvous point was halfway to the hospital at a grocery store parking lot.

A few minutes after we arrived at the parking lot, a couple paramedics appeared. I then, in disagreement, stumbled out of the car and into the ambulance. A taste of a cigarette seemed in order while I was being transported to the hospital. The medics informed me that if I lit one up the whole ambulance would explode. Apparently, I was not thinking about all of the oxygen tanks that were surrounding me and still did not seem to care. After proceeding to get rowdy, the medics threatened to pull the ambulance to the side of the road and call the police to deal with me. At that point, remaining calm was my only choice.

Upon arrival at the hospital, the medics quickly rushed me into the emergency room. I was immediately stripped down and was given one of those hospital paper outfits to wear. By this time, I was really "jones'n" for a smoke. The doctors told me no and that I just needed to lie down and relax. Obviously, I just couldn't take no for an answer. I told the doctor that I would walk through the hospital naked if that is what it takes to get a cigarette. Looking back now, that was rather humorous.

The doctor kept insisting that I stay in my place. This caused me to become more agitated. Finally, I stood up and threatened the doctor with violence, and made my way towards the outside, being determined to get that cigarette. To my surprise the doctor already had a back up plan. Two security guards, two nurses, and the doctor had tackled me to the hospital bed. I was able to fight them off for a brief amount of time. But, when they finally got me under control, they strapped me to the bed with me yelling and cursing at the medical staff. After noticing that I managed to break away from one of the straps, the staff also was quick to notice and had to hold me down again. Reflecting, I truly am sorry for what I had put that staff through.

Hence, here I am completely wasted, strapped down, and argumentative. Not to mention the fact that I was still "jones'n" for a smoke. The nurse began to run blood alcohol tests on me. When my results had come back, the nurse looked at me and asked "How in the hell are you still alive?" She said, "You should be almost dead, if not dead." My blood alcohol level tested at a 0.37. Keep in mind I was tested a couple of hours after being admitted in the emergency room.

My B.A.C. would have been higher earlier before arrival. My nurse was astounded that I was even awake and, yet, alone arguing with the staff. In the next chapter, I am going to show you a blood alcohol chart. You can gauge the different levels and stages of intoxication.

The nurse then proceeded to even the score with me. Because of the large amounts of alcohol that was in my system, I would need a catheter. The catheter was used primarily to drain out my toxic urine. Well, this nurse did not seem to waste any time at all. I cannot say that I blame her, now. She proceeded to grab my pride (penis) and then jammed this tube right through my pee hole. "Awwwwwwwwwww," I remember shouting. This was one of the most painful forms of well-deserved torture that I can possibly remember. Immediately after, she did what she had to do, my whole abdominal region felt like it was going to explode. That was definitely not a comfortable feeling in the least.

So, there I was laying their strapped down to a bed, with a tube in my pride. Would you believe after all of this I decided I was going to get angry and violent once more? I started to tug at the straps trying to break free again. I tugged so violently that the straps left indentations on my skin for months to follow. The doctors and nurses again ran into my room and threatened to call the police. At this point in time my family and a friend of mine had arrived. They came into my room and attempted to calm me down. My nurse had tried to sedate me. When she realized that it was not working she tried again. Finally, I passed out sometime after my second sedation.

Amazingly, I woke up some hours afterwards. The medical staff came into my room and told me that I was going to live. Still I was drunk, but calmer. The doctor decided that he was going to move me into a separate room. I was then unstrapped and escorted by security to my own personal cubicle. There were two security guards standing post outside of it just in case I became violent once more.

After some time a psychologist decided to enter my room, wanting to discuss the events that had led up to today's fiasco.

Also, he wanted to make sure that I was sane enough to leave the hospital. Well I fed him a bunch of lies and he saw fit for me to leave that night. Looking back now I was not in any shape to have left that place. The hospital should have kept me under observation for a minimum of three days because of my extreme condition.

Later on that evening, a friend of mine decided to give me a lift home from the hospital.

For the next few days I had to detoxify on my own. Doing this alone, without medical attention, is a very dangerous avenue to pursue. I was, however, fortunate enough that I did not have major withdraw symptoms. Aside from feeling violently sick and wanting to die, the shakes didn't seem all that bad.

A few days later after finishing my detox, I decided to check myself in to the local health department. Keep in mind I was completely broke and could not afford any kind of rehabilitation program. I sat down with a counselor and discussed my issues pertaining to alcohol. I explained my financial status to her. She must have seen how bad off that I was. I told her that I had been beaten by alcohol, surrendering the moment I stepped out of the hospital. She then proceeded to make a few phone calls. Luckily the state deemed it necessary that I get into a rehab facility right away making me extremely grateful for I did not have to pay a dime for my treatment. With this chain of events that unraveled, do you think that it was a coincidence? I don't.

I left for rehab the very next day and successfully completed a twenty-eight day program. After that month, my whole outlook on life changed completely. God and the assistance of rehab saved my life. My spirituality through all of those drinking years was almost gone completely. The events that took place that day in early February could only have been a work designed by God.

March 6, 2008

Day 28

Up all night to my roommate's snoring. Took shower and cig with hot chocolate. Had meeting and read my dear alcohol poem to the group. Eggs, sausage, hash brown. Played basketball and won first game of 21. Had meatballs and rice, fruit loops. Had my own farewell and everybody commented on my sense of humor in how I made everyone laugh their asses off. Getting ready for dinner. My counselor told me that someone who has left already has already relapsed and may not make it. Other people in the community also thanked me for helping them out and, especially, Melissa. Had dinner which was fried chicken and mashed potatoes. Had more meetings and a great presentation from a counselor who teaches on weekends. Watched the rest of "Guess"

Who" and a friend is awaiting my prank. He has been nervous all day long and the guys know it. It is freaking hilarious. The funny thing is I am not going to do anything at all and that is the prank. He is here begging me to tell him what I am going to do lol. Love playing mind games. It is so much fun. Packing my stuff up and know what is going on for tonight.

Even though I had forgotten about God so many times in my drunken lifestyle, He never forgot me. It was through my days in rehab, that I began to see the bigger picture of spirituality. I feel that if an alcoholic wants to survive, he/she must have some form of a spiritual belief. This disease will drain everything and everyone from you.

In closing, being alive today makes me a true miracle. I never thought that I would have ever made it this far. Every day I find there is something to be grateful for. When I was drinking, I was not grateful for anything or anyone. In my recovery, with the help of God, and other alcoholics, I will keep living my life to the fullest. For the still sick and suffering, I will always be there.

7

The Blood Alcohol Chart

Keep in mind that the effects of alcohol intoxication on a person individually can be greatly varied. Some people become intoxicated at a much lower level than others. Weight and tolerance play a factor in feeling the effects of alcohol as well. However no one is exempt from the amount of alcohol in their blood.

0.02~0.03 Bac

No loss of coordination-feeling of slight euphoria-loss of shyness-depressant effects are not apparent. You will feel mildly relaxed and a little lightheaded.

0.04~0.06 Bac

A feeling of well being-relaxation-lower inhibitions-A sensation of warmth-Euphoria-Have some minor impairment of reasoning and memory-Lowering of caution-Your behavior may become exaggerated and your emotions intensify.

0.07-0.09 Bac

Slight impairment of balance, speech, vision, reaction time, and hearing. Euphoria-Judgment and self control are reduced. Caution, reasoning and memory are impaired-Illegal to drive at this level. You may believe that you are functioning better than you really are.

0.10-0.125 Bac

Significant impairment of motor coordination-Loss of good judgment-Speech may be slurred-balance, vision, reaction time, and hearing affected-Euphoria-It is illegal to operate any motor vehicle at any level in all states.

0.13-0.15 Bac

Gross motor impairment and lack of physical control-Blurred vision and major loss of balance-Euphoria is reduced and dysphoria is beginning to appear-Judgment and perception is severely impaired. {Dysphoria} An emotional state of anxiety or depression or unease.

0.16-0.19 Bac

Dysphoria predominates-Nausea May appear-Drinker has the appearance of a sloppy drunk.

0.20 Bac

Feeling dazed and confused or otherwise disoriented-May need help to stand or walk-If injured, you may not feel the pain-Some people experience nausea or vomiting-Gag reflex is impaired and you can choke on your own vomit-Blackouts are likely to occur.

0.25 Bac

All mental, physical and sensory functions are severely impaired-Increased risk of asphyxiation from choking on vomit-Seriously injuring yourself from falls and other accidents.

0.30 Bac

Stupor-You have little comprehension of where you are-You may pass out suddenly and be difficult to awaken.

0.35 Bac

Coma is possible-This is the level of surgical anesthesia.

0.40 Bac

Onset of coma and possible death due to respiratory arrest.

(The Police Notebook-University of Oklahoma)

Alcohol for some people can be used as a way of relaxing. Other people may enjoy alcohol because of the taste. Some wine and other liquors tend to go well with certain meals. Many of us just enjoy the effect that it brings to us. Alcoholics however may enjoy all of these, as well. We become dependent upon it.

People who drink alcohol always run the risk of becoming an alcoholic. However, some people are more susceptible than others. Scientifically it is still a mystery. Generally speaking, alcoholism seems to be more rampant among those with a family history of it. Even though statistically it may run high in families with a history, I know of people who have acquired this disease without alcoholism in their lineage.

It is a disease that does not discriminate. It does not matter if you are black, white, Asian, Spanish, rich or poor. You could be young, old, male or female and alcoholism will gladly friend you. There are many emotions however that an alcoholic will experience. Many of these, no doubt, a person will eventually experience throughout the course of their life time. However, most of these emotions alcoholics will experience everyday. These emotions will be much more intense for the alcoholic. In this chapter I am going to discuss some of these emotions and how they affect a person with alcoholism.

Picture the game show "Wheel of Fortune" to where we, the contestants, spin the wheel in hopes of winning cash and prizes.

For the alcoholic who still suffers, I am going to call this game the "Wheel of Misfortune." As we keep spinning and playing the game every day, we yell out letters in hopes of eventually solving this puzzle. Instead of money and prizes on the wheel, try to envision emotions on the wheel. Each and every day that we wake up we will spin this wheel. As we give the wheel a heave and a hoe it goes around and around and it lands on several different emotions such as denial, ego, isolation, self-centeredness and fear. We may also land on a free trip. The free trip is a day free of emotional turmoil for the alcoholic. This of course is a rare occasion. Obviously we do not want to land on the bankrupt space. Being emotionally bankrupt was the scariest feeling that I had ever encountered. After some time we had finally decided that we were ready to solve the puzzle. We then yelled out alcoholism. To our amazement we are correct but there is no celebration. In real life however for the active alcoholic, there is no solving the puzzle without help. Most of us will not make it to the bonus round. This is a serious and most deadly disease and not a game. Although there is no cure, there is a way out. I will be discussing the recovery process in a later chapter. I now want to move on to a few of these different emotions.

I am going to start with *fear*. What is fear? Fear is a plague that affects millions of people throughout the world. It mostly remains reclusive in my life now but it is always ready to rear its ugly head. I did not realize, for many years, my biggest battle was the fear that I had inside of me. It is what mostly drove me deeper into my addiction. Many alcoholics become afraid of change. Some may have had something that happened to them in their past. They sometimes are afraid to speak about it.

At times, they may feel that nobody would understand or could ever help them. So, consequently, they will drink continuously to numb their pain and hide their feelings. Often times alcoholics like me would be scared of screwing things up all the time. I would fear what others thought of me. The fact of the matter is that many alcoholics live in this frightening state of mind. There are many factors that play into this nightmare.

Growing up I was always critical of me. When playing sports, I would always try to perfect everything. I refused to come in second place. Many people would say that is a great attitude to have and indeed this may be. What was driving my desire for perfection was my fear. What happens if I come in second? What would people think of me? What would my family think?

I had always felt pressured for some reason. I suppose that some of this had to do with how I have always felt different from others. I just never felt normal. I guess that it just made me want to prove myself more and more.

There are, of course, healthy fears and unhealthy ones. I began at a young age shouldering my unhealthy fear. This seemed to have catapulted onward throughout my life of drinking. Many alcoholics and drug addicts carry this defect. We sometimes use, simply to run away from our uncertainties. This is unhealthy because our problems come back increasingly worse when we sober up.

I have had many unhealthy fears in my lifetime. They had grown so bad that I would fear going to public places without the assistance of alcohol. I was always scared of rejection.

In my past relationships with girlfriends, this would hold true. I would often split up with them before they had a chance to leave me. I had a fear of what her friends would think of me. I was frightened by commitment. I became scared of me and lacked self-confidence. I was afraid that when a relationship had become more serious, I would drink and then mess everything up. This of course was something that I most certainly did do. I would often dread the thought of losing my job and then my girlfriend. Maybe that could be a healthy fear. The notion of losing my job was constantly on my mind. This was more prevalent in my drinking days.

I often thought that by drinking, my feelings of fear would subside. They would vanquish temporarily, but would present themselves again the very next day. This of course had caused me to binge drink. The more days in a row that I could remain drunk, I figured the better off I would be. I was very lost in my mixed emotions. Fear was always at the top of my list.

I would often worry about my past catching up to me. What if someone that I roughed up a while back decided to come after me? I had seen this happen to people before so I was cautious about where I would hangout. Many times, when I was younger, I couldn't remember parties or places that I had been. I would have frequent blackouts after being so heavily intoxicated. Who is to say that I didn't cause harm to people that were at these places?

The next fear that I am going to discuss is one that most people have after they leave their favorite watering hole. It's the thought of getting caught behind the wheel intoxicated. This happens to be a huge concern for alcoholics. Obviously, problem drinkers and alcoholics will drink and drive more than the average person. Let me just say that driving to the liquor store in the morning with a case of the shakes is scary. Because of the alcohol that was still in my body from the night before, I most certainly would have been locked up. It also doesn't help when you still smell like a brewery.

My ultimate fear now is picking up another drink. Alcoholism is a progressive disease. If I were to consume an alcoholic beverage now I would start off worse than where I stopped. God knows that I was in such a horrible condition when I quit, that I can't even imagine worse. Death was literally knocking down my door.

Fear was taking over my life and became my God. I had almost completely succumbed to this frightful state of mind. It controlled every aspect of my decision making process. Can you imagine living day to day with this black cloud hovering over your every thought or action? This emotion can be so powerful and so paralyzing. It had brought me to my knees on many occasions.

There were times when I would just break down and cry. The emotional toll that it took on me was just indescribable. I would never wish this disease of addiction on even my worst enemy.

I would become anxious about the after-life. Being someone who was and is of Christian faith, naturally I would shudder at the thought of going to hell. It is sometimes funny when I reminisce. The only time that I asked for God's help was when I had a nasty hangover or had some other kind of drunken illness. Upon lying on the hospital bed almost dead, I found God once again. It amazes me now to know that God was always there for me, but I was never there for him.

Change was something that, as an active alcoholic, to which I was not very receptive. The thought of trying something new or going down an unknown path made me very uneasy. Why? I guess that I was at ease and comfortable to a certain extent being a drunk.

The fact of the matter is that many alcoholics live in this anguish. I now want to move on to discuss self-centeredness.

Self-centeredness became the core of my existence. I would love to point my finger at everything and everyone. In my mind it was hardly ever my fault. I enjoyed playing god. When things did not go the way I had planned, I would become angry and begin acting like a child. Becoming very selfish, I would gladly help my self before I would help others. These actions of course led me into isolation.

Isolation is by no means healthy for anyone, yet this is most dangerous for the alcoholic. I would often alienate me from the rest of the world. I didn't really care about anyone or anything. Often, I just wanted to be left alone. Sometimes, there was an attitude that the world revolved around me and that others must stop what they are doing and divert their attention to me. Alcoholics many times tend to want everyone to cater to them. When we do not get our way we sometimes tend to dwell in our self pity.

I personally wasted enough hours in my own self-pity. I would often ask my self questions like: Am I ever going to do something with my life? Why can't I just be normal? Why can I not drink like a normal person? These were questions that would depress me. I would sometimes sit down with a bottle and cry myself into a drunken slumber. This thought process is juvenile in nature, yet, very dangerous as well. These thoughts may lead some alcoholics to inflict harm to themselves physically. All of these emotions could eventually lead into suicidal tendencies.

My feelings as a lush were never stable. If my life depended on it, I could not stay organized. One minute I would want to take a drive and then the next I would want to go to sleep. Some days I would wake up happy and excited but as soon as something did not go my way I would become angry. Most people can turn their anger on and off like a switch. Usually this anger will dissipate in a reasonable amount of time. But alcoholics like me would let this inconvenience ruin their whole day. My emotions were all over the place. The painful truth is even if the alcoholic is not drinking, the feelings remain.

Being an alcoholic does not mean that you have to be drunk around the clock. Many people have a false interpretation of who an alcoholic really is. You could be an alcoholic and not have had a drink in months. The fact is if you are truly an alcoholic, without help, you will come back for that drink. Your messed up emotional state of mind will stay with you also. The only difference is when you drink your feelings become amplified. Being sober to me involves more than just taking the drink away. It also means staying mentally focused. I constantly have to work daily on my character defects.

Ego becomes a huge factor that can also play into many alcoholics lives. I have personally met other alcoholics who were wealthy and very successful. After time they had lost almost everything they owned. Their ego had played such a devastating role in their lives. Some were business owners, school teachers and doctors.

One person in particular stands out in my mind. This person's ego was so high that I don't even think N.A.S.A. has the capability of tracking it. This person was very successful and owned a couple of businesses and was always hanging out with famous people. Nevertheless, he was all about his status. Addiction does not care about your status. This man thought that if he didn't use then he would no longer be with the "In crowd". Instead of taking care of himself, he was more worried about what other people thought of him rather than fixing up him. He just did not want to give up his self-indulged lifestyle. Important things to him were using his manipulation skills to get women into bed. Hanging out with all of the famous people and delving in the perks was seemingly more pertinent to him. His ego had gotten the best of him. Despite a brief amount of clean time, he went back out using again. Having lost all contact with this person, I have no idea if he is still alive. Hopefully, he finally surrendered and is alive and doing well. I may never know but I wish him the best.

For years denial had also kept me drinking. Blaming others for my problems, I never seemed to come to terms with my own addiction. I did not want to believe that I may actually have issues with alcohol. Sure, having more frequent blackouts and picking fights was normal, Right? Some people do that all of the time.

Maybe even drinking before work could be a bit extreme but people do it.

Denial will keep the alcoholic active in his or her drinking career. Eventually the alcoholic will need to come to grips that he or she has a problem. Like my self, most of us had to hit our bottom. Unfortunately a lot of us never get to our bottom because we pass away before we hit it. Many of us will let our pride and egos blind us to who we really are.

Here is an example of what the alcoholic goes through mentally. Picture a campfire in your mind. As you envision this fire you notice that the flames are dancing. Much like in an alcoholics mind the emotions are constantly fluttering. Now, what happens when you add gasoline to the fire? The flames will jump up and become very flammable and dangerous. The same principle holds true when an alcoholic takes a drink. Alcohol fuels our character defects much like how gasoline fuels fire.

In conclusion there are many emotions that an alcoholic will experience. I could write a whole separate book on those. I feel that all of them are equally as important. But, my goal of course is to share with you the emotions that I had battled with daily as an active drinker. These emotions, when ignited by alcohol, almost ended my life. I will always be carrying these with me. The amazing part is that I now know how to deal with them without drowning them in the sauce.

"I sought the Lord, and He answered me; He delivered me from all of my fears." **Psalm 34:4**

8

The physical consequences that I had endured over the course of my drinking really took a toll on my body. Although every person's physical chemistry is different, generally they will have many of the same reactions to alcohol.

During most of my drinking years my goal was to get drunk. Euphoria was a feeling I just loved. Many people refer to this feeling as a "buzz". I was on top of the world with this sensation. Often times I just felt immortal. This mood, for me, was one to be desired frequently. I was able to leave my self for a while. It always helped to lower my inhibitions. After some time, I was no longer ingesting for the "buzz;" I was doing this because I physically had to.

Alcohol had begun masticating away everything that I may have had on my stomach. This in turn would make me most hungry at times. I am sure that some of you have had a case of the munchies before. I always preferred greasy foods to control my alcohol induced famine. Tacos, burgers, or a cheese steak would always hit the spot. Munchies were commonly a consequence of my boozing. Further down the road when I became really driven by alcohol abuse, I would not eat for periods of time. I was drinking so much that at times I didn't even think about food. Sometimes I would pass out way before the desire to eat would even show up. Because alcohol would take its effect more swiftly and powerfully, I would usually consume it on an empty stomach. Blackouts became more frequent.

Blackouts were something that I would experience from time to time. For those of you, who may not be familiar with them, allow me to explain. Blackouts are brought on by increased amounts of alcohol that will ultimately affect your memory process. Think of this as temporary amnesia. In some cases they can become permanent. Let's say that you went out drinking one night with some friends. The next day you wake up and had forgotten what you did. You may even have forgotten where you were. You may decide to ask your friends what happened the night before because you cannot seem to remember. This is a classic case of a blackout.

Blackouts are not a laughing matter. Some people get violent and do things that they would not normally think of doing when they are sober. This is very problematic for a number of reasons. Sexual encounters, fights, accidents, murders, robberies, and many other terrible things have been known to occur during a blackout. The best bet is to stay away from consuming large amounts of this drug. Even though knowing a limit for an alcoholic is unheard of, you should keep in mind that large amounts of this over time will produce health issues.

While drinking, I used to read the surgeon general's warning on the bottles of beer. I would always snicker at these comments:

"Warning: This product may cause health problems." These warnings always seemed so redundant to me. Everything that I looked at seemed to have a health warning of some sort. Eventually I would finally heed this warning. I found out that it really was not written for my sheer amusement. Not until I became sober did I realize that it was not humorous at all. In my early stages of recovery I found that I did have some health issues. Many alcoholics develop stomach ulcers, liver problems, kidney problems and dental problems. Others will experience permanent brain damage (wet brain). Since being sober, I have found that I do have some stomach problems and a dental issue that I did not even know about. I even realized that I was lactose intolerant, as well. These problems had started and existed for quite a while. I was too drunk and numb to notice that many had been there all of that time, while others were from the consequence of boozing.

I am sure that most people have had a run in with a hangover at some point during their drinking escapades.

Scientifically, no one really knows for sure why we receive this punishment. Some scientists believe that it may have something to do with your blood sugar, family history, sleeping patterns, and much more. The fact is that they really suck. Some people hardly ever have hangovers, and more power to them. I always had them and they were most brutal. They can produce sweating, shaking, vomiting, upset stomach, headaches and dizziness. All of these symptoms can, also, occur in succession. I was the victim of all of these at the same time. Hangovers always made me lazy and moody . . . as if I wasn't moody enough.

There are cures for a hangover though. One way to get over one is to drink lots of water and wait it out. I usually decided to go another route. Considering I was impatient and a full blown alcoholic, I would drink them away. I strongly suggest that no one try this. It is very dangerous and may lead directly to alcoholism.

Eat something!!! I was a huge fan of greasy foods when I was hung over. Anything spicy would make me feel better. During my final days of drinking, my hangovers had become increasingly worse. They would begin to last for three days or so. Eating food at that point did not seem to make me feel any better. My body was going through serious withdrawal symptoms.

Double vision is another symptom of alcohol abuse. By consuming too much alcohol can result in seeing double. I am sure that most people who have had a rough night of drinking have experienced this. I should have been the poster child for double vision. Alcohol affects nerves in your brain that control your eye movement. It will slow your brain enough to where your eyes will have a hard time focusing. While in this state you may become nauseous. I obviously would not recommend getting behind the wheel of a vehicle at this time.

Often times after binge drinking, I would experience many fits of anxiety. I would drink to escape the everyday stresses but when I returned sober they always came back three fold. When these bouts would hit me, my heart rate would increase. Many times my heart would pound hastily and arduously for a complete day. I was always cautious about eating sugary foods. Whenever I would consume caffeine or candy, my heart rate would climb as well. With this being said my anxiety level would escalate higher. I never really understood why I would physically go through all of this. I believe that some of these symptoms were derived once more from withdrawing. Furthermore, other issues of anxiety would vary. I would get nervous and sweat as well as get dizzy and shakey. Anyone who may have anxiety issues could more closely relate.

I would often have periods of sadness or depression. For really no good reason, I would begin crying. Recollecting on past endeavors of misery never helped the situation either. Often I would just sit alone and listen to music. I would isolate myself from the rest of the world. Something very tiny in terms of sadness would immediately heighten itself to a whole new parallel. Similarly, the smallest of any occasion, I had the ability to escalate it way beyond what it should be.

Finally, fatigue and the overall feeling of lethargy would set in. During and after bouts of drinking, my body would become exhausted. Many times it would just decide to shut down. Even though mentally I would push my body to keep going, physically it said no. After days of hurried activities in a drunken stupor, I would become very drowsy. This carried many consequences. It affected my productivity at work. I became sick and lost more days from work. Often I would walk around like a zombie for days on end.

At one point I had a rather lucrative job. It was a very demanding and stressful managerial position. I had put in fifty to seventy hours a week. This job alone would have fatigued anyone without the assistance of alcohol. Keep in mind I now had a full time drinking schedule, as well as a job. This would always cramp my drinking time. The two would always battle each other daily. All the same I did, however, find time to get drunk. I remember some days when I would have already worked ten hours, and was ready to pack it up. I would then receive a phone call informing me that I needed to be at another location within the hour. I would then have to work another eight hours on top of my previous ten.

Whenever I would get a day off, I would hit the booze extra hard. Why not? I deserved it after all of these long hours. Right? I would start drinking first thing in the morning and it wouldn't stop until I passed out. Usually this was late at night or early the next morning. I figured that you can't drink all day if you don't start in the morning. Consequently, I lost that job because my life had become seriously unmanageable.

The human body takes beatings mentally and physically due to the abuse of this drug. I am sure that there are plenty more physical consequences that I have not listed. Generally speaking every person's body reacts in a different fashion to alcohol. As a result of my stories, alone, I hope that this proves beneficial to whoever may be inquiring about alcoholism. I keep emphasizing this is a serious and most deadly disease.

9

There are many ways that alcoholics will hide their booze. In this chapter I am going to go over the reasons why and how we keep it hidden.

Some alcoholics can come up with the craziest ways of hiding their alcohol. Drug addicts, likewise, may also follow the same routine. When I was younger I would hide my booze because (A) it was illegal to be drinking under age in the first place and (B) from my family and others.

Alcoholics and problem drinkers a like have many reasons for concealing their habits. Some drinkers will hide it so their significant others will not know exactly how much they are really consuming. I have seen this happen plenty of times. Guys tend to keep it hidden from their wives or girlfriends. I have also seen mothers hiding their booze from their children.

When I was a teenager, my family had a billiard table in the basement of our house. My friends and I were avid pool players always in search of a place to shoot.

We had the option of shooting pool up the street at a local pool hall, and pay, or play for free at my house. Occasionally, we would go up the street to the pool hall. Afterwards, we always seemed to end up at my house. Now in order for any of this activity to take place we needed one thing. That small thing I am quite sure that you have guessed was alcohol. We all would pile into a vehicle and visit our favorite liquor store. Sometimes we even had to play "Hey mister" if the clerk didn't serve us.

Once we had gotten our booze, we would sometimes pop by the local pool hall. My friends and I would sit outside in our vehicles and get lit. I found that drinking before shooting pool just made me unbeatable. After a couple hours of shooting we would normally wrap it up and head back to my house. We were however wise to my parents sleeping habits. Comically, we had developed a plan to sneak our leftover booze into the house.

All of us were athletes and we would tend to bring our sports bags wherever we went. Many times my friends and I would leave our bags in our vehicles. We had all decided that concealing the alcohol in our sports bags would be an excellent idea. By taking the booze out of its brown paper bag and positioning it ever so carefully in our sports bag prevented the "cling clang" noises. Well we always worked together as a team to reach our goal. The goal was smuggling the booze into my house without my folks ever knowing.

In this particular house that I was living in at the time had a basement, 1st floor, 2nd floor, and two back porches. My folks slept on the second floor above the driveway, unfortunately. This was where we had to park our vehicles. We always did run the risk of my folks hearing us pull up. More than likely we already had the booze in our bags and were ready for action anyway. We all would make a decision on who was going to be the "runner". The runner of course was the person who would grab the sports bags full of booze and stealth it to our hiding spot. Whoever was left among us would have to enter the house at one of our doors. I swear this was just like a comical military operation. "Operation Booze" Our hiding spot for the alcohol was underneath one of our porches. However the porch that we needed to crawl under was beneath my parent's window. As you may now see, whoever was the runner had to be extraordinarily quiet. Underneath the porch a ways was a window leading into the basement. This window was very small yet large enough to fit alcoholic beverages through. Directly in front of this window on the inside was my pool table. This was a perfect set up for drunken teens.

Anyway, while the runner was doing his job, the rest of us would pick a point of entry into the house. We had to be extra cautious with any noise that we would make because my folks had dogs as well. We would normally choose the front door. Reason being is if my parents happened to be awake then they would see us coming into the house without booze. Secondly we also served as a distraction for the runner. The runner would always stay put underneath the porch. He would wait for us to give the all clear from the basement or the "My parents are awake" signal. Given that my parents were sleeping at this point then we would unlock a door to the house for the runner. If by chance my folks were awake then the runner could just come in through the front door after the booze was stashed. Once the plan was executed then we would all meet in the basement.

At this point we would rack the pool balls and start shooting. Carefully we would unlock the basement window and grab our choices of poison. Since I always had a CD player in the basement, we would turn the volume to low and begin the party.

Some time during these nights, my father would wake up and venture to the basement. He always knew that we were up to no good but he kept to himself. We had mastered the art of hiding our booze when we heard him coming. Looking back now it was just hilarious on how we were stricken with panic. We would hear the floors above creaking and instantly we were all over each other trying to hide the alcohol. If you can picture the game "Musical Chairs" then you may have a good idea of what I am describing. Instead of everyone circling around chairs we would circle the pool table. Obviously none of us had wanted to be the one caught with a beer in our hands.

As we were drinking we would stash our empty bottles back into our sports bags. Many times we would become so lazy that we would just toss them underneath the porch. We of course had to dispose of the evidence right? Well we had executed this plan successfully throughout our teenage years until one particular summer day.

I was awakened one morning to the sound of hammering. I had gotten out of bed and went outside to see what all of the commotion was. Fear had stricken me when I realized what was taking place. My father and brother in law at the time were tearing apart the graveyard (the porch). I had suddenly remembered that my friends and I had forgotten to clean up all of our empty beer bottles (dead soldiers). We all had apparently gotten side tracked and it slipped our minds. Suddenly, our dog had come running out from underneath the porch with a beer in its mouth. The dog had since punctured the can and beer was spraying everywhere. This crazy animal had proceeded to drink the beer and was drunk shortly there after.

Great! My folks were now onto us. Fortunately for us, the damage had already been done. There were so many dead soldiers underneath the porch that it took forever for me to clean that mess up. I must have gone through eight big hefty bags that were designed primarily for yard work.

Not being stupid, my folks realized that my friends and I would drink occasionally. They did not know however how much we were drinking. The look of shock or astonishment if you will was priceless. At least at this point in time my friends and I were now coming of legal age anyways.

As the years went on and my drinking habits had worsened, I began finding new ways of hiding my addiction. Once again I remained a huge fan of my sports bag. I had begun making a habit of carrying it with me wherever I would go. This usually would hinder any suspicion that may have been aroused by family members.

I would use the bag to sneak alcohol in and also out of my house as well. I had a cabinet drawer in my room that only I had a key to. This is where I would stash most of my alcohol. In high school my friends would pull into the driveway and park. I would often fill and then lower my sports bag full of beer from my bedroom window. My friends would grab my bag and stash it in their vehicles. I would then simply walk right out of the front door with my parents not even knowing.

Other ways that I would stash varied primarily on the current situation. Let me say that chewing gum and eating mints did not work very well. Drinking vodka to disguise my breath did not work for me either. Now on occasion I would mix my whisky into a coke or Pepsi can. This worked for me in a couple ways because it was easy to conceal and it tasted great. Gatorade bottles I would utilize for vodka and other clear liquors. I personally did not enjoy the mixture of the two because of the awful taste. Flasks of course are another way to carry your booze. Obviously by doing this, you are announcing to the world that you are a drunk.

Some years later I was living with my sister and she always had liquor lying around somewhere. I would often wake up in the morning with the shakes or just a nasty hangover. Her vodka was the most accessible to me and rather appealing most mornings. If you have ever been hurting similar to how I was, it was a godsend to have alcohol around. I would often drink most of her vodka. Afterwards, I was careful to remember just how much of it I had consumed. I would then fill up absence of alcohol with the water.

My sister did not drink her vodka often so I knew that this could work until I could replace the bottle.

When I was really desperate, towards the end of my drinking career, I found other places to hide my booze. At this time I was drinking pretty much anything that I could get my hands on. I would take my daily morning trip to the liquor store. We all know those people who stand outside of their favorite retailer in the morning. Usually you find hordes of them on sale days waiting for the store to open. They are all getting ready to bum rush everyone in their way. This was me in the morning outside of the liquor store. Looking back now it does make me chuckle a little.

Anyhow, I would buy my concoctions and drink a couple on the way home. I made sure that if I was going to buy beer that I would also purchase whisky. Beer was more acceptable sitting in my family's refrigerator than whisky. In order for me to sneak the whisky in the house, I would have to conceal it on my person. If it was cold outside I would hide it in my jacket pockets. During the warmer days I would hide it in my waist band, covered by my t-shirt.

Often I would go on three or four day benders. I needed to maintain enough alcohol to keep me going. Waking up in the morning feeling like death really sucked. So the first thing on my mind was that I needed a drink and fast. With careful planning I would have stashed just enough alcohol in my room from the night before. This way in case my shakes were really bad, and I couldn't drive to the liquor store, I would have enough alcohol to fix my self. I would stash my booze in my closet or underneath my mattress. Sometimes I would stash my pints in a pair of old shoes sitting around. Another great place to stash were access panels in the walls of the house. I used to hide bottles in the vents of the house. Who ever looks in the vents right? I would also, on occasion, duct tape a whisky bottle underneath the toilet tank lid. That was a great spot yet risky. I had discovered many places to stash my alcohol. I am sure that there are many others for the alcoholic who still suffers.

The bottom line is if you have to hide your drinking, then you may have a serious problem. Going to extremes to hide my addiction was never fun. It was necessary.

10

To ask for help can be one of the hardest things for an alcoholic. Pride plays a major factor as well as denial. Some alcoholics realize that they may have an issue with alcohol, but because of their pride, they attempt to fix themselves. This is of course a most dangerous route to take. Obviously if we could fix ourselves, then we wouldn't be alcoholics.

So on and on the alcoholic goes, attempting to find a way around receiving help. They begin to repeat the same pattern over and over again. After numerous struggles the alcoholic will always wind up back in the bottle. This method of thinking is called insanity.

There are three different categories of drinkers. Many people seem to be confused about the differences between a social drinker, problem or heavy drinker and a dependent or alcoholic drinker.

First, a description of a *social drinker:* Someone who can have a drink or two and possibly more, but knows when to stop. They can go on for long periods of time without a desire or compulsion to drink. Social drinkers may enjoy a tasty glass of wine accompanied by a steak or whatever their favorite dish may be. Others may enjoy a refreshing cold beer while performing yard work. Some may even enjoy their favorite import at a sporting event or at a social gathering. The point being is that they can control how much they drink and know when to stop.

Second, the ***problem or heavy drinker:*** This person enjoys drinking until he/she gets drunk or "buzzed." You may know of someone who fits this profile. Perhaps, you do. I once held this title years ago. The problem drinker can be seen at all the aforementioned places, just like a social drinker. There is, though, a difference between the two.

The problem drinker will consume many more drinks then everyone else at the event he/she attends. Usually, this person will get loud and obnoxious. He/she sometimes has a reputation for starting fights, being lewd, drinking and then driving, shoplifting, vandalism and making other poor decisions. This drinker sometimes enjoys being the center of attention (life of the party). Remember, being a heavy drinker could cause somebody to develop into an alcoholic. A problem drinker is bad news!

Finally, ***the alcoholic:*** Similarly, these irrational behaviors my hold true to the alcoholic, as well. But, after time, an alcoholic becomes dependent upon alcohol, as I was. For years there has been debate over just how a person becomes an alcoholic. The fact is that nobody really knows for sure. Some scientists have said that it gets passed down through genetics from generation to generation. I believe that this is a factor. Still, many alcoholics have not had any kind of family history of alcohol abuse. Heavy drinkers statistically are more prone to get this disease than social drinkers. While some people develop this disease at a very young age, others may not become dependent until they are in their seventies. There have been many studies performed throughout history and nothing has been conclusive. It is a very mysterious and baffling disease.

Alcoholism is a devastating, progressive and incurable disease. After an undetermined amount of time, one could fall victim to alcoholism. This disease does not discriminate. A person's age, gender, race or status does not hold weight to this affliction. There is hope, however, with proper treatment. Alcohol itself is only a symptom of this disease. Psychological and spiritual aspects complete the treatment. If an alcoholic were to abstain from alcohol completely, he/she will still suffer emotionally, as well as spiritually. Alcohol to me is but only an allergy that triggers the emotional, physical, and spiritual turmoil.

There are others who would challenge the fact that alcoholism is a disease. But, everyone is entitled to their opinion. Conversely, most of these people are completely ignorant to the facts. It is impossible for someone to understand alcoholism fully if they have never walked in our shoes. A number of people have written books and articles about how they stopped without the assistance of anyone. If you are a true alcoholic, you will need help or you will eventually perish from this disease. These are the simple facts. I do, however, applaud those who have kept abstinence from drinking and that they do whatever it takes to remain physically sober.

Most alcoholics, like me, would drink excessively to blanket feelings, even though, I always knew that it was only a temporary fix for my many emotional issues. Drinking caused me to forget emotions, such as fear, guilt, loneliness, anger and stress. This led to my body being physically dependent.

Did you know that just fewer than 13.8 million U.S. adults have some kind of issue with alcohol? Out of this number, 8.1 million suffer from alcoholism. Also, a staggering half of a million U.S. children, aged nine to twelve years, are addicted to alcohol. I do not know how you may feel about these statistics. I find them rather disturbing.

(2009Drugandalcoholtreatment.centers.net)

For those of who do not currently suffer from alcoholism, try to imagine living without drinking any liquids. What would happen to your body physically? Similarly, picture yourself driving a car that is low in fuel. What happens when the tank is empty? The obvious answer to both of these questions is that they will shut down. The same principle applies to that of the alcoholic's body. The alcoholic becomes physically dependent upon booze, much like gas to the engine and water to the non-alcoholic.

Addiction: A physical or psychological need for a habit forming substance. This will most likely be drugs or alcohol. In physical addiction, the body adapts to the substance being used and then gradually requires an increased amount to reproduce the effects that were originally produced by smaller doses.

(The American Heritage Science Dictionary)

Alcoholism: It is a chronic disease characterized by a strong craving for alcohol. There is a constant or periodic reliance on the use of alcohol despite adverse consequences. The inability to limit drinking, physical illness when drinking is stopped, and the need of increasing amounts of alcohol to feel its effects.

(NIH-National Institute on Alcohol Abuse and Alcoholism)

Many of us had never been truly sane throughout our drinking days. Those of us, who have been in recovery, can now understand our once ill past. Insanity is not isolated to just alcoholics, it also holds true to people without problems with booze or drugs. For instance: Some people will go to work everyday with a chip on their shoulder. Sure they will do their job but they carry this negative attitude about them. They will begin to wonder why their co-workers do not get along with them. Day after day and month after month, this person continues in repeating the same cycle. Their co-workers will keep their distance the best that they can. Nothing ever improves between their relationships. Now the person with the attitude keeps wondering why they keep their distance. This is a prime example of insanity. Insanity also plays a factor into someone who may be in denial.

Alcoholics are notoriously known for being in a state of denial. I used to think that if I limited my alcohol intake then I would be fine. Some of us would think, "Well, that person drinks more than me but still can get up and make it to work the next day." "I must be doing something wrong if I can't do the same". "I don't have a problem and I am going to figure out how to drink like them." On and on we go blinding ourselves from the truth. I would not listen to anyone. Talking to an active alcoholic is like talking to a wall. I would get extra defensive when anyone tried to offer their help. Unfortunately most alcoholics much like me have to hit their bottoms first. What is so very scary is that many of us die before we reach that potentially pivotal moment.

The alcoholic who is finally sick and tired of being sick and tired may ask for help. There are many resources readily available for someone who is need of help. When I was an active drinker I did not realize that there were services available, outside of rehab and alcoholics anonymous. I am going to list some resources that are available for the alcoholic as well as anyone who may be interested.

First, I want to start with the community health center. When I was beaten badly by my alcohol abuse, a decision was warranted. Was I going to continue drinking myself to death or will I seek help? I had to suck up my pride before deciding to ask for assistance. A rehabilitation center was my answer. Before I could enter a rehab facility, I needed to get evaluated first. Therefore, I drove to the local health center. They proceeded to give me an evaluation to see if I was suitable for a rehab facility. After the counselors talked to me and ran tests, they decided that I was a prime candidate for rehab.

For those of you who may desire to inquire about help for a family member and/or friends, the health center is an important first step. The cost of testing may vary from state to state. The center should provide out-patient treatment programs, as well. For those of you who cannot afford rehab, these programs are offered for a fee.

Second, I want to discuss the rehabilitation programs. Once you have completed your testing with the health center counselor and they deem you a candidate for rehab, you have a choice. When choosing a rehab, money and location will always play a factor. Luckily for me the state took care of my expenses. For those who have medical insurance, check to see how much your insurance provider will cover. Most insurance companies, though, will only pay a small portion. Nonetheless, something is better than nothing. Choosing a rehab that is best suited for you can be a challenge. Counselors, though, should be able to steer you in the right direction. They may ask about your finances in an effort to place you where it is most financially feasible for you.

I will say that not all rehabs are located in the best of places. The alcoholic must also understand that they themselves are not exactly in the best of places either. For some of us at least rehab has a bed and food. Many of us have been court ordered to attend a rehab of the states choosing. This is fine because at least you have the opportunity to change your life around.

Pay attention once you are in rehab. Get as much out of this place as you possibly can. This could ultimately change the course of your life for the better. Stick with the program and put forth the effort that will be required. My counselors in rehab were recovering alcoholics and drug addicts. This of course just made it so much easier for me because they all could relate to exactly how I was feeling at any given time. These people had been in my shoes before. Although rehab was tough, it was one of the best involvements that I ever experienced. Embrace the time that you spend there, and the wealth of knowledge you will acquire. You will be getting a second chance at life. For some it may be a 3rd, 4th, or 5th chance. Just try to be grateful because many of us do not even get a second chance.

Third, I want to discuss the *12 step program*. Alcoholics Anonymous as well as Narcotics Anonymous are always available if and when you may want to attend. These programs have proven to be very beneficial in assisting the addict in staying sober. The great thing about these programs is the fact that they are free. As an addict you can choose to go to either one. You also have the luxury of going to both if you choose. If you want to get better you must abstain from all use of alcohol and narcotics. There is no cure for addiction, but these meetings are the best medicine.

For me it was imperative that I get into one of these rooms. I desperately needed structure and balance in my life. These programs teach you everything that you need to know about living a sober life. I highly recommend these programs to anyone who may be suffering from addiction. When I left rehab, I already had a structured plan. I was going to attend 90 meetings in 90 days. I eventually got through those three months and I stuck with the plan. For me that was a miracle in itself. I figured that if every day I was able to get out and get a drink, why couldn't I get out and get a meeting. I had to break my unhealthy habits and replace them by going to meetings. Now before I reached my bottom, I was bouncing in and out of A.A. I never really felt like I belonged there because these people in my mind were worse off than me. I just could not bring myself to admit that I was an alcoholic. I had tried to take what I learned in these meetings and incorporate this knowledge into my drinking. I was trying to find a way to control my drinking. I did not follow what was suggested to me in those rooms. so, needless to say, I found myself in the hospital a year later fighting for my life.

Being clean and gratefully sober, I thank A.A. for being a staple in my life. It is a wonderful and yet simple program. There are a couple ways that you can find A.A. or N.A. meetings. If you have access to the internet you can Google them. Then just follow the steps to lead you to local meetings. Your local health center can also provide you with pamphlets. This will give you a whole list of all the meetings within your county. Some churches and hospitals may also carry these pamphlets. Local rehab facilities are also another resource at your disposal. If you happen to know of anyone in these programs, I am quite sure that they will be more than willing to help you locate a meeting.

Other resources that you can use to acquire about these programs can be found in various ways. Books, magazines, and television programs are also a great resource to use. The yellow pages should have a crisis hotline that you can call. This hotline will put you in touch with someone from A.A. or N.A. I my self had reached out to the hotline before. Someone from these programs will talk with you and may take you to a meeting if you want.

Last, but not least, I want to say that help will always be there. The only requirement for you is the desire to get help. I had to suck up may pride and I found the strength to surrender.

Like I have said before I was just sick and tired of being sick and tired. Please do not hesitate to find help.

11

Anyone, who makes it to the recovery process, has encountered a miracle. Most addicts have never had the luxury of experiencing the beauty of recovery. In this chapter I am going to share my wisdom on this subject. Everything that I will be discussing is a reflection of the path that I took and that I still do take towards my recovery. Whenever there is another alcoholic in need of help always be there for them. When you are, it will always benefit you as well. I still remember the people who threw me out a life line. I want to be there for others who desperately need one as well. This helps me to remain sober. I will begin to remember how tough it was for me. The pain that I went through will never be forgotten. I never want to go venturing back down that road. I acquire my gratefulness simply by reflecting on my horrific past. By doing this I also scare my self straight.

There may be great experiences as well as bad on the path of recovery. My aim is to not sugar coat anything but to educate you. This will be a tough and challenging road. At the same time it can be fun and rewarding. In my early sobriety I would often wonder if I could actually have fun doing the same things that I used to do when I was drinking. I can now answer that as a yes. For years I had conditioned my body to enjoy certain events drunk. The same principle holds true in sobriety. You can condition your self to enjoy some of those events sober now. The difference now is that I can remember all of these events.

Many changes are going to happen to you physically and mentally in early sobriety. Some of these changes may be temporary or permanent. This of course may depend on many factors. For instance: How long were you abusing your drug or drugs of choice? How often were you using? What kind of activities did you participate in while using (Sharing needles, unprotected sex)? Memory loss and short termed memory is not uncommon during early sobriety. However in some cases permanent short termed memory can occur.

When I was in my first month of recovery, my stomach was in bad shape. For years I was used to eating primarily unbalanced meals. While I was in rehab I was being fed three squared meals a day. When sobering up this became a shock to my body. My digestive system seemed to have been confused. After some time though my stomach problems seemed to work themselves out for the most part. Dental issues may also become a factor. For some alcoholics and addicts their teeth had been rotting for quite some time. This is mostly due to the lack of self care. High amounts of sugar in alcoholic beverages can also contribute to this. Many do not even realize it until they become sober. The alcoholic's gums can become very unhealthy. Gingivitis may have been taking effect and you now just start to realize it. There are many more health issues that you may encounter in early sobriety. I knew people in early sobriety like my self who never even had a clue that we were already experiencing health problems. We were to busy being drunk and numb to even notice. What I want to discuss now is a strange phenomenon that happens while you are sleeping. This strange and mysterious occurrence is called drunk or drug dreams. These dreams can be scary yet beneficial at the same time. While sleeping, you begin to dream about getting drunk or high again. These dreams are usually very vivid and true to life. I often would experience these dreams four to five times a week in my early recovery. I would often wake up in a panic, and begin to look around my room to make sure that there were not any empty bottles lying around. These dreams would often have me at a party with a drink in my hand. At the very beginning of these dreams I would always have a buzz. I would then proceed to pound beers and then start feeling guilty afterwards. In these dreams I would think to my self, wait I just blew my sobriety. Panicking even more, I would finally wake up.

These of course can be rather horrifying as you can imagine. On the same token they can be very beneficial. When I would finally wake up and realize that it was just a dream, I became grateful that I was still sober. For my first six months I had experienced many of these. After some time though, they began to slow down. Now they are not as frequent. I may experience about one of them a month. Just remember that these are perfectly normal.

If you want to remain sober there will be persons and places that you will need to make adjustments with. I personally know of so many people in early recovery who started hanging out with their old drinking and drug buddies. Some of them never made it back. There may be way to much influence and temptation for you to handle. Just remember that this is not a game. This is life or death. It is imperative that you stay away from old drinking and drugging buddies. However, if these old pals are in recovery then that's perfectly fine. I know that some people may be married to someone who still uses. This of course makes things a lot more complicated. I am not going to give marital advice for I am not qualified to do so. I do know however, in early sobriety, making arrangements to live somewhere else for a while is not a bad idea.

Bars, crack houses, hotels, strip joints, may have been the spots that got you in trouble in the first place. Some of these people that you need to stay away from you can always find in these places. Sometimes it could be your house though. Some people may need to stay away from their homes or even their towns for a while. Maybe perhaps you have to go back home because of financial circumstances. Even though this may not be the safest place for you to be, it can be done. Having a sponsor could prove to be very beneficial for you in this particular situation. I will be discussing sponsorship in another chapter.

In my early sobriety, I took different routes while driving my car. Seeing the local watering holes or liquor stores could be a trigger for you. You may start to crave for that drink or drug while you are passing by. I remember when I was around six months sober, I was in a really foul mood for no good reason. Keep in mind this will happen a lot in early sobriety. Anyway, I was driving down the highway and was fast approaching a street that I knew very well. This street was home to my favorite liquor store. This was the kind of store that would stay open practically all night and would open early as well. I was debating in my head on whether I should just stop or to keep going. For a brief moment all that I wanted to do was get drunk. Luckily while I was debating this in my head, I had just passed that street. Well that made my decision a bit easier and I had decided to keep going. My point is some of us may need to drive a different route to minimize our triggers and maintain sobriety. Sometimes you have to do whatever it takes to keep you sober. Remember that your life depends on it.

Hanging out with sober people is your best bet in early recovery. Perhaps you may have met some people in rehab or at meetings. If you have not attended any of those places that's fine also. Look to hangout with people who do not drink or drug. This will help you in learning how to live life and have fun on sober terms. Your risk of temptation should lower in the process as well.

For me in early recovery, I hung out with people who were in the same boat as me. This proved to be very beneficial. After time I had established a comfort zone. I knew that if I needed anything I could rely on these friends. Unfortunately, I couldn't say the same about my old drinking buddies. After some time I began to feel comfortable being around people who do drink. I would advise not hanging around establishments that serve alcohol in your early stages of sobriety. After time you will develop your own comfort zone.

There is an unwritten rule for people in early sobriety. It states that in early recovery one should stay away from an intimate relationship. Giving yourself a year to get in touch with your own emotions before you take on a relationship is advisable. If you already happen to be in one then there are Al Anon meetings for your significant other. These meetings provide loved ones an inside view of what us addicts go through. They also teach loved ones on how cope with us.

This rule I did not follow. I had jumped into a relationship as soon as I had gotten out of rehab. Consequently, I found my self very upset and depressed. I almost went back out drinking. Sure everyone has a different view on this rule but I first hand understand the importance of it. My legacy of bad relationships remained true even after I had gotten sober. I had spent years of destroying my self and relationships a long the way when I was drinking. Just getting sober, I never gave my self the time to straighten my head out before I had jumped into another one. We simply cannot repair ourselves mentally in a brief amount of time. This takes a lot of work.

We must keep ourselves busy and active. For some of us we just spent years of drinking and drugging and destroying ourselves both mentally and physically. Now it is time for us to build ourselves back up. Early sobriety could be the most exciting and yet most challenging time of your lives. To assist in getting ourselves back in order and to maintain our sobriety, I am going to list some helpful tips.

I have found that writing out what I am feeling relieves tension and stress. Go and get yourself a pad and some paper. When you become agitated or someone has upset you, just write it out. After you are finished writing, toss it away if you would like. For me this is a fantastic way to vent.

Keep your mind active by reading. Reading books on recovery and spirituality are always helpful. Some may prefer religious readings like the bible for instance. Either way, you should want to educate your mind. Now is the time to learn as much about your disease as you possibly can. By reading up on this condition you will have a better understanding on how to treat it.

Now, we have gone over reading and writing, I want to discuss exercise. Seeing as I was once an excellent athlete, exercise has always been easy for me, though this does not always come easy for others. Maybe some of you have rarely ever exercised. This is not a problem at all. The point is exercising does wonders for your body both physically and mentally. By engaging in physical exertion, your brain releases chemicals called endorphins. Endorphins are feel-good chemicals. For me these guys provide me with a natural high. After a little exercise, I will almost immediately begin to feel better mentally. My stress level will drop and my cob webs will dissipate from my mind. The other benefit to exercise is that you will physically begin to feel and look better. This can boost your confidence as well as keep you in good health. Some of us spent years destroying our bodies. Let's start building up again.

There are many places to go for exercising. A local track at a college or high school is great for running. Perhaps you may enjoy a nice walk through your local park. You can also learn how to enjoy nature again while striding through the outdoors. Some may prefer going to a gym. The gym can be an outstanding place for exercise. Lifting weights and doing cardio will work wonders for your body. Most gyms will have personal trainers that can assist you. Usually when signing up for a membership, you can get free lessons from a personal trainer. Take advantage of this if all possible. They can evaluate where you are physically, and get you started on a routine. Some of us just do not have the money to join a gym. There is no need to panic because you have other options. Exercising at home can work wonders as well. Pushups and sit ups can kick off those endorphins all the same. If you have internet access, you can look up exercise routines. If all possible, get yourself a structured daily routine for exercising. This has really helped me through my recovery process.

Meditation is another stress reliever. There are many different forms of meditation. I am going to list a few that seem to be very effective in early recovery. Some people prefer yoga as a way of relaxing their minds. Others prefer acupuncture or Pilates. Any of these forms of meditation can be beneficial in relaxing the mind and body. Other people like my self prefer a more conventional way of meditating. I enjoy taking nature walks as well as watching the wave's crash on the beach. There is just something of therapeutic value, when I can just sit and stare at the ocean. It seems to help me relax and clear my mind.

I also take pleasure in praying as another form of meditation. When I have private time away from everyone else, I cherish the time talking to God. This is where I can just hand over all of my worries to God and let him shoulder them. There is something that I had finally learned after all of these years. Simply it is to let go and let God.

Going back to spirituality once more, I had to acquire a spiritual plan to maintain my sobriety. Everyone needs to be hopeful as well we all need help. This is true for everyone and not just alcoholics. However alcoholics seem to need a bigger dose of spirituality than others. Most of us had spent our lives in the bottle and feeling like there was no hope for us. There is hope but we have to believe. It was imperative for me to take a walk of faith and put my hopes in God. I know that many people do not believe in God or the Christian faith. Some people may have a different interpretation of God. Many believe in the stars, Buddhism or some favor nature or even some favor nothing. The important thing is that most alcoholics have to have some form of spirituality to stay sober. The *12 step program* can further lead you in the right direction towards finding your spirituality.

Having a proper diet in recovery is very important. For years my diet was just horrible. I had spent days on end hardly eating to days of eating nothing but junk. Being in a drunken state at times would usually trigger my want for a greasy, heart stopping, burger. Occasionally, I did however favor a spicy, fattening, taco. There were times though that I would get so famished that I really didn't care what I ate. Three meals a day was almost an unattainable goal in my days of boozing. My body was very nutritionally deprived before I made it through the doors of rehab. After I had left rehab I was fifteen pounds heavier. These were of course pounds that my body desperately needed. It is imperative that you get yourself on the right track eating three square meals a day. I would seek advice from a doctor. Eating healthy will benefit you greatly physically and mentally. This will also simmer down your mood swings that will occur in early sobriety. In early recovery I had ferocious cravings. The depletion of alcohol from my system seemed to confuse it. The alcoholic's body will begin to demand alcohol but we choose not to ingest it. This in turn will develop our bodies to crave it. A single craving for me would usually last for a brief amount of time. For my first six months of sobriety they were frequent. The cravings for me caused physical discomfort. My heart would race and anxiety would begin. I would become very restless and I couldn't sit still. Mentally my mind would begin to wander. I would begin to fantasize about how nice it would be to have a drink in my hand. These cravings can be extremely dangerous if one acts upon them. Please do not give in to these cravings because your life may depend upon it. This is simply your disease encouraging you on. Rest easy though because eventually they will slow down. Fortunately there is a way to battle off your cravings.

For those who are not diabetic, eat some sugary candies. Whenever you feel a craving coming on, eat a piece of chocolate. Jolly ranchers and lollipops worked well for me in early recovery. I would drink a lot of hot chocolate and tea. Ice cream is still one of my favorites even though my body does not agree. I am not sure exactly why sugar seems to calm down the cravings. My best guess is that alcohol was packed with sugar so our bodies may be looking for that replacement. Either way I will stick with what works for me. Just remember to keep all of this in moderation. It does not matter what kind of healthy diet that you may be on, you can always squeeze in some sweets.

Now, let me discuss intake of nicotine and caffeine. Cigarette smoking as we know can be potentially dangerous. However, if you are still a smoker in your early recovery, you may not want to quit just yet. I know that this may sound like terrible advice to some. Try to understand that quitting one addiction at a time is hard enough. The ceasing of drinking and drugging in itself is extremely stressful both mentally and physically. Halting the use of nicotine will only add more of a burden on you. For me smoking seemed to calm me down especially when I was craving alcohol.

After you begin feeling comfortable with how you are dealing with your sobriety, then quitting is always an option. I was told by many people who have had a lot of sobriety, as a general rule, to keep smoking for at least another year. I am not going to suggest that anyone do this, but the task is to find your comfort zone. For those of you, who do not smoke, that's great. Please do not start.

I have used the word moderation in this chapter already. When it comes to caffeine and candies use moderation. Caffeine especially in early sobriety should be used at a minimum. Sometimes I found in my early stages that too much caffeine only brought on cravings. I am not sure exactly why, but I believe it was because it would make me feel jittery. Sometimes if I were to get jittery I would get anxious. This in turn would make my mind race. Anxiety would take over and my heart would begin to beat faster. This would pose a problem because the only way that I knew how to calm my self down was to drink alcohol. Try to understand that in early sobriety you will have enough anxiety and stress to learn how to deal with. Just like everything in life, try to use moderation.

The road of recovery can be very challenging. This road is not always paved in gold. Life is going to happen whether we are sober or not. At least, being sober gives us a great chance at living a normal life. When we are drinking and drugging we have a very slim chance if any. Life for me, now, is much more valuable than it ever was. Take each step of your recovery with the utmost care. Our lives are valuable and should never be taken for granted. By reading and understanding this chapter, you may be able to put these suggestions into motion. Just as important, my next chapter I will be discussing relapse and prevention.

12

So many people that I know have put the drugs and alcohol on the shelf, but they stopped working on bettering themselves. Alcohol and drugs are only symptoms of our disease. We must be constantly working on improving mentally. Sure, I quit drinking. But if I stop working on changing my behaviors then there is a struggle. A "dry drunk" is a person who only abstains from the use of alcohol. This person typically will still behave in the same fashion that they did while they were drinking. Many times this person will be miserable and will, eventually, drink again. If the mental and spiritual aspects of this disease are not worked on daily, then the chances of staying in recovery are low. Sobriety is the daily work of your mental, spiritual, and physical aspects of this disease.

This disease of addiction is a life time battle. It will eventually kill you if you stop putting forth the effort to keep yourself sober. Unfortunately, some people that I knew in early sobriety indulged again and lost their lives. I know of people who had been sober for seven to eight years and went back out. Our disease is always progressive even though we may be sober. This simply means that if we start drinking or using again, we will start off worse than when we stopped. This disease is just waiting for us to slip and then consume us whole. The reality of this can be very frightening.

I have decided to share some more ways of coping with this affliction. Relapse and prevention is of extremely high importance.

Now this is where you can move on with your life while you trudge the road to happiness.

Life comes at you fast especially when you are sober. Most of us for years did not realize that life had always been excelling at a quickened pace. The reason most likely is because we were to busy being drunk or high. Once we begin sobering up we may notice that the bills are still there. Our health may not be exactly where it should be. For me all of these applied as well as the loss of a loved one. I knew that this person had passed away but I was so lost in my addiction that I had missed the funeral. I would miss holidays as well. On the bright side of it all I can now be present and sober. I can also remember events now instead of having blackouts. There will be plenty of things that life will throw at you while being sober. We do not have to drink or drug over them anymore.

I have learned many things along my road to recovery but one acronym has always stuck with me. *H.A.L.T.* simply means hungry, angry, lonely, and tired. When my life begins to become overwhelming for me all that I have to do is H.A.L.T.

After getting into a funk, I will ask myself if I am hungry, angry, lonely or tired. For me as an alcoholic I can be rather moody at times. Usually the reasons for this have to do with H.A.L.T. This is when I go back to where I was discussing three square meals a day. As alcoholics we tend to go back to our old habits. I will sometimes miss meals and, in turn, making me moody. It is imperative to get three meals a day.

If I am angry at someone or something, I sometimes just need to halt. For years I would lash out at people, criticize them or yell and scream. I could sever someone in half with just my tongue. A big part of being sober, now, is to act human. It must be understood that for years many of us hurt people in countless ways. It is time that we take responsibility for our actions. When we become angry, walking away can be rather beneficial. Writing out why we are angry on a pad and paper works wonders, too. Always try to remember to halt.

Loneliness is not pleasant. For alcoholics, being lonely can be hazardous. Many of us like me did the most drinking when I was lonely. The good news is that we do not have to be alone any longer. There are plenty of A.A. or N.A. meetings in which to go. You can always call your sponsor or a good friend. Praying proves to be very effective as well. Every so often, when I am feeling lonely, God shoulders my weight.

Tired is the last word in H.A.L.T. Let me explain. When I am extremely tired, my mind begins to wander. I would begin the "stinkin thinkin" phenomenon. For an alcoholic this is bad. When I was actively drinking, half of the time I was physically and mentally exhausted. I had become accustomed to mixing alcohol with fatigue. In turn this had become a habit. When I am tired, my mind will remind me of how nice it would be to have a drink. The drink will help me relax me. Right? I do not intend on finding out. That's for sure. While in early sobriety, get plenty of rest. I try to catch at least six to eight hours of sleep a night. I know my body needs nurturing. Always get into a healthy routine. Remember, when you think you want to drink, ask yourself if you are hungry, angry, lonely, or tired.

I have discussed Alcoholics Anonymous, as well as Narcotics Anonymous, in an earlier chapter. Let me suggest how to get a sponsor. It is through these two programs that you can acquire a sponsor. A sponsor is someone who has at least a year of sobriety and has worked all of the steps that these programs offer. These steps are a guide that many of us should follow in order to get sober and remain sober. You can learn more about these steps in a meeting and even rehab. Having a sponsor can be most helpful for you in all stages of your sobriety. It is suggested that one has a sponsor in early sobriety. Many have asked, "How do I get a sponsor?" There are several ways one can go about it. One of the easiest methods is to sit down at a meeting and listen to people tell their stories. If you hear someone's story that may sound similar to yours, then ask them if they are sponsoring. You, of course, will have to feel comfortable being around this person. One thing to keep in mind is that men sponsor men and women sponsor women.

Many benefits can come from having a sponsor. Anything that you may be feeling or going through, you can always share with them. His/her job is to steer you in the right direction. Expect to have a certain amount of work thrown at you. Just because you may be sober, does not mean that you are well. Alcohol and drugs as I have said before are only a symptom of your disease. At this point, you must learn to live life on life's terms. This is where the real work begins. Having a sponsor can literally save your life. Remember that sponsors have been through what you have been through and sometimes worse. They all are recovering alcoholics or addicts. You can take comfort in knowing that you are in good hands. You may even acquire a lifetime friend. There may come a time when your life is changing and may be moving in another direction. It may become necessary to dismiss our current sponsor and acquire a different one. This is perfectly fine because your goal is to keep yourself sober and to be living happy.

There are going to be times when we will just feel easily frustrated. Everything will just get on our nerves. Maybe we will begin to feel extra defensive. This is all normal for we had a history of hiding these feelings behind a mask of booze and drugs. Now is the time to face these feelings head on. I used to be so negative. I would say things to myself like, "Things never go my way." or "Why should I even try?" or "My life sucks, but it's not my fault." I had to free myself of these defeated attitudes and change my mind set. Changing my negative thoughts to positive ones has helped me out tremendously. Instead of me saying that, "My life sucks and it's not my fault." I would tell myself that, "Sure, I have had some set-backs, but I am a strong person and will get through this." When I would say," Things never go my way.", I would tell myself that, "I am going to try to make a difference and never give up." When," Why should I even try?" comes around, I tell myself that God has something in store for me and all that I need to do is stay positive and take baby steps. Having a sponsor and going to meetings can alleviate or help control negative thoughts. It is of high importance to sobriety that we do this.

There will be times when people may treat you in a disrespectful manner. Even worse some people may discriminate against you. Just because you may be sober now, that does not mean that everyone will be as accepting as you may wish.

When I was in early sobriety, I had managed to get one of my old jobs back. Things were beginning to go well for me. I was very productive and led my staff. The lack of trust was still there from my former co-workers. I had worked there for a year and was never reprimanded, not even once. I showed up on time and was early on many occasions. Despite all of my hard work and genuine efforts, I was terminated.

I was accused of breaking company policy. This, of course, was all fabricated. That was an emotionally hard blow for me to swallow. During that year, my boss had developed a suspicion of me drinking again. This was not the case by any means. I did have personal issues that I was dealing with outside of work. My car would not start because my battery had died. I needed time to have the new one installed. But, I was unable to replace the battery until I got paid a few days later. I asked for rides to work but no one was available to take me. I even asked my boss and co-workers if they would pick me up. At that point, I was so broke I could not afford a cab. At the same time, I had to be out of my house in a couple of days. I was in the middle of a move. Needless to say, I had to take a few days off without pay. Given my past, my boss naturally assumed that I was on a bender again. I really did not have a choice. He of course assumed that I was drinking again. I did provide a receipt as proof that I had a new battery installed in my car. Even though, I do not believe that he was ever convinced. The company had terminated me later without a valid reason.

Anyway, my point is that people may never trust you again. This is not your problem. It is theirs. As long as you remain genuine and do your part, the pieces will come together. Always stay true to yourself. Whatever people may say or do that may be demoralizing to you, remember that this is their issue not yours. Sometimes people may be jealous of you. Many have problems with themselves and decide to belittle you. That in some way makes them feel better. Forget about these people because you have to worry about you.

Stay away from too much isolation. If you suddenly become bored or antsy all by yourself, get to a meeting. Sometimes meetings may not be feasible. You could always go for a walk or a drive. You should also call your sponsor because that is why they are there. The key is to keep your mind active. There is that old saying, "An idle mind is the devil's playground." This was definitely the truth for me and it still is.

I am the kind of person that, given too much isolation, could talk myself into trouble. Every now and then, we just need to kick our own butts up and out the door. I find that reading a book or working on a puzzle is a healthy form of isolation. I am a believer of challenging the mind. Studying more on the disease of addiction is a great way of spending your alone time. The last thing that I want personally is to be caught in the web of isolation. I had spent plenty of time there over staying my welcome. This was my last phase of drunkenness that almost took my life. Just be cautious of how much time you spend alone.

I now want to talk about honesty. For years many of us lied, cheated, stole, manipulated, and just down right deceived others. We almost molded our whole existence around dishonesty. Many of us would have done almost anything to get our way. Similarly we would have done almost anything to get our next drink or drug. This is the time to turn our lives around. We must practice being honest. We should begin by being honest with ourselves. This of course is not always an easy feat. If we reflect on how and what got us to our all time lows, then it should become obvious to us.

Asking you questions about yourself is an important step. Say for instance, "Why didn't that relationship with Sue workout? Was it really because she bothered me or was it because of my drinking that made me so temperamental? Was my drinking more important to me?" You may have thought that your boss was a real stickler. Ask yourself why was he a stickler? "Maybe he was acting that way, because I was always late. Perhaps, it was because I called out of work every other week?" If you can, go back and think of all the times that things did not work out in your favor. Think of lost jobs, relationships, D.W.I.'s, fights. Be honest with yourself. "Was my drinking and drugging, the root cause of all of this?" Most likely, your answer will be yes. Because of drinking and drugging for periods of time, your personality will begin to change. When you wake up everyday, try practicing honesty with other people. You will find that after practicing honesty, people will respect you more. Similarly, people who remember you at your worse will begin to see changes in you. Today, I am grateful that my family is still around. The best part is they all were able to see me get sober. I now talk often with my parents and we have a much healthier relationship.

Changing behavior will take some time though. Practicing honesty with others, as well as yourself, may be tough at times. Bear in mind, that we are not perfect and we will fall short at times. Trust can be earned by showing other people that you have changed. Words are not enough for most people. People want to see words put into action. Keep in mind that certain people may never come around you again. All of the pain and destruction that you caused during your drinking days, may have been more than enough for them to handle. If this is the case, then accept this and move on. Keep practicing honesty and you will start to feel better about yourself. Your outlook on life may greatly improve. Just remember to put your words into action and the rest will fall into place.

Finally, we all need to do something special for ourselves. All of these things that we practice to keep ourselves sober weighs heavy at times. Go have some fun in sobriety. Do some things that you use to do in the past before you became a wreck. Maybe an amusement park would suit your fancy. I personally enjoyed riding roller coasters in my early recovery and still do. Perhaps buy yourself a new outfit. Dressing up and looking good can always boost your confidence. You could always try to do something that you have never done before. Learn to speak a new language, play an instrument, write poetry, take a road trip, visit museums or aquariums, see movies, go bowling, or whatever works for you. The best part is you have a choice now. You can have all kinds of fun without the use of drugs and alcohol.

Life for me has become so much easier, now that I have remained sober. Sure problems are always going to be there, but that's life. As I have said before, we have to live on life's terms. We cannot control everything that life throws at us. I know that it can become very tough at times but I just "Let go and let God." By doing this a huge weight will just lift off my shoulders. Many of us have lugged this load around for so long and now it's just time to be free.

13

March 7, 2008

Day 29

Woke up. Took a shower and shaved. Took my sheets off of the bed and threw them in the hallway. Finished the rest of my packing. Cig and hot chocolate and had morning meeting. I closed the meeting and grabbed my breakfast. French toast, eggs, bacon, hash browns, my favorite. As soon as I sat down to eat, my dad showed up, so I quickly ate some bacon and grabbed my stuff and said farewell to everyone. Drove my car to McDonald's. Dad got a coffee and I, a Coke. Went home and checked my cell and unpacked and checked my messages on computer. My phone blew up with everyone calling me. That was great, at first. But, then frustrating. Went to a meeting in Chestertown and it was great. Told everyone my situation and we went to lunch at a pizza joint afterwards. Went home and my cousin, Erik, brother, sister, niece, folks and Chip and Terri showed up. We ate pizza and wings and then I went to see my friend, Carol. She was extremely apologetic about what had happened. I am still a little bitter, but I am not jumping into anything quite yet. I have my own issues.

In this chapter I am going to briefly discuss some of the obstacles that I had to overcome in the days of early sobriety.

Shortly after I left rehab, I needed to find a job. Because of my lack of job stability, I was very worried. I had many delinquent bills needing to be paid. This was, obviously, a result of my having been so intertwined in my addiction. Even though I was sober, the world just didn't pause and wait for me to play catch-up. I decided to make some contacts with old friends and landed a job. The pay was much lower than what I had expected but this was a much needed lesson in humility. After some time, I began excelling far beyond what I thought I was capable of. Some of my family had decided that they were going to make a move to Florida. Due to this circumstance, I then had to move from where I was staying and in with other family members in Maryland. I, however, was not exactly happy or comfortable with this move, yet I did not have a choice. Eventually, moving day had arrived and I packed all of my stuff and claimed residency with other family members. Luckily, this move was only a few miles away; thus allowing me to keep my job. Unknowingly, there were other plans being made for me at my job. About two weeks after getting settled into my new residence, my employment was terminated. Unjustly so, I might add. I was now unemployed and with no source of income. Having to explain this predicament to my family was very nerve racking.

Imagine not being able to pay bills and trying to pay rent without a job. Shortly after this loss, I contacted unemployment. They needed me to explain why I lost my job. At that point, I didn't really know how. My employer never gave me a legit reason as to why. I guess that I can thank the good ole state of Maryland for allowing employers to terminate someone with no valid reason. Either way, I had my suspicions. Thankfully, the government decided to grant me unemployment compensation. The amount of funds that I was receiving was not enough for me to make all my payments. I had to scrape by, along with trying to find a job. On and on I went, month after month, and I never landed an interview, yet alone a call back. I had applied online to jobs that were not even in my field. Showing up to businesses to fill out an application never worked either. The response that I would always receive was, "Go somewhere and fill it out online." You know it's amazing how times have changed. Years ago, I could just walk into a business and fill out an application and sometimes speak with someone on the spot. Anyway, my family began to get aggravated with me. They assumed that I was going back to my old ways and that I was not trying hard enough.

I was constantly harassed about paying rent. How could I have done so? All along, my living conditions were not the best either.

While I was staying with my family in Maryland, the economy began taking its toll on them, as well. Dealing with life's problems without the assistance of alcohol was a new concept for me. Let me just say that it was very mind boggling. Where I was staying, at the time, my family members seemed to drink to forget their problems. Alcohol became the primary source of every argument we had. Even though they knew I was sober, the drinking for them did not cease. I had multiple discussions with them concerning my thoughts on this matter, but to no avail. Eventually, I had to come to grips with myself. Realizing that I was the one with the drinking problem, not them, made it a bit easier for everyone. Could they have been more considerate? Sure. They could have, but all the same, I was the one with the addiction. In spite of this,

I did manage to stay sober by going to meetings and keeping myself occupied in a healthy way. Keeping my mind busy by reading benefited me enormously. As well, I would de-stress by lifting weights and exercising. Because of being unemployed, I was around the house a lot. No doubt this did not help with preventing little tiffs here and there. But again, what could I do?

In time one of my family members had lost their job as well. Here we are with three of us in the household and only one of us had a job. Now, you can only imagine the arguments that took place along with the stress levels. Shortly thereafter, I had to make another move, as well as, my other two family members.

Once again, I packed my things and drove route 95 south to Florida. I had some family who were living in Ocala. Ocala was central to almost every major beach. Still unemployed, I had decided to try my luck in a state with much less opportunity for work than Maryland. But, again, what choice did I really have? Living on the streets did not seem very favorable. While in Florida, I also attempted to try the armed forces. They turned me down because of my past love affair with alcohol. Staying with my family seemed to be my best bet.

Having the sunshine and a change of atmosphere felt wonderful and my living conditions seemed to improve as well. I spent many hours on the golf course improving my game. My game, as you can imagine, became much better. The best part of this Florida stay began two days after I had arrived. The events that took place next could only have been an act of God.

On my second day in Ocala my nephew and I decided to head downtown. We were debating on whether we should shoot some pool or go see this band that was playing at a local restaurant. The music we heard in the street began enticing the two of us. Our decision at that time became an easy one. We began walking through the streets and entered this restaurant that neither of us had ever been. The band was playing on the top deck of this establishment, overlooking the city. As we made our way through a certain hallway, I had glanced over at this crowd of women walking past us. Suddenly my eyes took notice of this beautiful, yet familiar looking, woman. My pulse heightened and my heart jumped. Hastily and without almost no hesitation, I called out her name. She stopped dead in her tracks and we then locked eyes. She was a friend of mine from years ago. We had dated back in Maryland when we were much younger. After some time, we had split up and went our separate ways. We lost contact with each other and had not spoken in over twelve years. We, immediately, hugged one another. Since my nephew was with me, an introduction was made. Quickly, we began small talk and exchanged phone numbers. Come to find out, this was the first time that she had ever stepped foot in that establishment, as well. Coincidence?

I think not! The funny thing about that night is we never did get to see the band play.

A couple days later, we met at that same restaurant and began catching up on the years past. She explained to me that she had been married for several years and divorced. That was what brought her to Florida. I explained my predicament to her. She then decided to pull some job strings for me. By her recommendation, I got an interview and landed a job. I know that God had brought the both of us back into each other's lives. This was all part of His plan. Day after day I had prayed for God to help keep me sober and to put the right people into my life. Even with all of the arguments in Maryland, including my financial strife, God always kept me on my feet. He helped and still does to keep me focused and to never give up. Anyway, we started dating again and it lasted for a few months. Things just became too complicated and we decided to remain friends. Even though things did not work out for us, I'am still a better person for knowing her.

My new job was working for a major retailer. This put me back in my comfort zone working loss prevention. Quickly, I made new friends with my immediate co-workers. I really enjoyed my job, even though I was only getting 30 hours a week. Finding a full time job in Florida was no easy task. Having a job period, after a year of unemployment, was a blessing in itself. Along with the excitement of being employed, I would spend the days I had off by visiting other towns. Orlando, Clearwater, Daytona, and Madeira Beach were a few to name. Again, serenity for me was standing on the pier and the beautiful white sands of Clearwater. Watching the waves crashing into the sand only to recede and to repeat all over again, was comforting to me. Here I could put all of my worries on God's shoulders. In those moments my gratefulness of having a second chance at life was most high. God opened up my eyes to see a beauty that far superseded my loneliest of times. It was and still is moments like this, I will forever savor.

After some time, my family had decided that they wanted to move back to Maryland. This of course put me back into a mental spiral of emotions. Here I was finally employed, yet alone a second job as well, and now I have to pick up and leave again. Part of me wanted to stay in Florida, yet part of me wanted to come back to Maryland. Yes, I was torn between. The one thing I knew to do in this situation was to ask God for His guidance. Where God wanted me to go was where I was going. Being obedient to God's plan, however, is not exactly an easy thing to do for an alcoholic. I just have to trust that He is making the right choices for me and I will obey. After all, if God could pull me from the depths of my addiction, who am I to veer off the path that He is laying down before me? Well, I began to follow God's plan and He led me back to Maryland. I did, though, attempt to stay in Florida, but I was unable to afford it.

When I landed back in Maryland, I had stayed at my brother's place for a few months. He was overseas at the time and actually trusted me enough to watch over his house and dog. I never saw that coming . . . haha! During this time, I again made some contacts with old friends seeking employment. And again, God had answered my prayers. A friend of mine landed me an interview and I got the job.

In closing, my life now is so much easier than ever. I no longer have to wake up worrying about what I did the night before, nor do I have the constant fear that I use to. I have learned to live life on life's terms. The best part is that I have gained trust back from my friends and family. I have become more reliable in every way. I, do, however, have to constantly work on my emotions. This is a lifetime process and it cannot be taken lightly. I work a full time job and I am going back to college in hopes of finishing my degree. Since I have been following God's path and staying receptive and obedient to Him, my life has drastically gotten better. Always remember that early sobriety can be tough, but for me staying sober without God would have been impossible.

I was given a second chance at life and am going to run with it. I will not pretend to be immune from this disease. Some days, for me in sobriety, can be very tough. I will take my toughest day in sobriety over my happiest day in drinking. It is time to learn how to love myself and others again. We should not take every day for granted. I will be forever grateful that I received a second chance.

Remain sober and happy today, because we are not promised tomorrow. It is important to take our sobriety one day at a time. We are all in this together. We cannot do this alone. Remember to utilize the programs that are at your disposal. I hope that what I have written may help you along your journey. If I can make a difference in just one person's life, then I have accomplished what I have set out to do. I have now carried my message and I will continue to do so. I hope that others will do the same. I wish much peace and sobriety to everyone trudging this road to happiness.

Don't quit five minutes before the miracle happens.